St. Louis Community College

Library

5801 Wilson Avenue
St. Louis, Missouri 63110

DINING IN-ST. LOUIS

DINING IN-ST. LOUIS

J.A. Baer II and Cecile K. Lowenhaupt

Foreword by Vincent Price

PEANUT BUTTER PUBLISHING
Peanut Butter Towers · Seattle, Washington 98134

Cover Photography by Dale Windham

Copyright © 1979 by Peanut Butter Publishing
Printed in the United States of America
ISBN 0-89716-045-2

First Printing December 1979

CONTENTS

FOREWORD

Backstage at the Muni Opera a few years ago, crumpled in my disguise as Fagin, I would sit and hear with joy that rousing opening chorus of young voices singing "Food, Glorious Food." I love that musical, I love the Muni, but most of all I love the memories of good, yes, glorious food that comes wafting back to me whenever I hear that song or think of St. Louis, in my youth and now.

The wondrous list of restaurants and recipes in this book proves my contention that St. Louis is a good eating town, and my memories prove that it always was. I must confess that the theatrical schedule, such as my recent visits to St. Louis has imposed on me—no dinner before a show, and only a few places open after one a.m.—may tend to make the eating memories of my youth more reliable than my present experiences, but I have dined with joy and pleasure in recent years from the Arch to Clayton and round about in a good many of the restaurants mentioned here.

St. Louis bears out my contention that the civilization potential of a city (or country) can be measured as accurately in its kitchens as in its museums, centers of learning and concert halls. The cookery renaissance that has swept America in the past few decades did not, perhaps, have as painful a rebirth in St. Louis as in some places, for its food was never ordinary and the exciting ethnic mixture of my home town has always made its eating habits varied and adventurous.

I remember with love and jumping taste buds Joe Garavelli's wondrous spaghetti and German cookies at Christmas from Busch's Gardens (now Busch's Grove.) On the South Side, French and Creole cooking in friends' homes on the other side of the River Des Peres, and, of course, most of all the wonders of our table at home. Find a man who loves to eat well and you can be fairly sure he learned it at the family table or his mother's apron.

Not that my parents didn't appreciate the arts per se—with four artistic children, they had to—but, rather than art, Mother collected recipes and treasures to make her table more attractive; tourism, wherever my folks indulged in it, was in truth more a question of smell and taste than sight and sound. Our house was suffused with the intriguing aromas of my Mother's culinary experimentations, "sniffed out" during her exploration of menus from other parts of the country and the world. It made our home a joy for us and a treat for our friends and none of us has led a dull gastronomical life, thanks to her caring education of our palates.

When I visit my home town today I am always amused and pleased that my friends think highly enough of me to bombard me with equal enthusiasm with information about what's going on at the Museum or the Symphony Hall—and where's still the best place to eat, or where to try some new delights, some charming new approach to the art of dining!

Sum it up by saying that this wonderful city offers so much to its inhabitants and its visitors that this book by Cubby Baer and Ceci Lowenhaupt is a welcome guide to one of the city's greatest offerings—the bounty of its tables. It is always good fortune to dine in St. Louis—it is good fortune indeed that we can now not only dine out with assurance of high culinary satisfaction, but "dine in" as well with a heightened potential for culinary adventure.

Vincent Price

Being something of a globe-trotter—and harboring an impassioned interest in good food—I am frequently called upon for restaurant guidance. Since that time just after World War II when the world began to travel for fun, friends have asked for my special list of restaurants in famous capitals, as well as those off the beaten paths. When asked to write this book, I took another good look at my own home town. Long known as the Gateway to the West, St. Louis is middle-America in all respects, a potpourri of nationalities: French, Italian, German, Polish, Greek and more. It is, as well, traditionally a city of home entertainment where "dining in" has always been the rule rather than the exception. And along with home dining, good restaurants have been part and parcel of St. Louis's history, dating back to the Planter's Hotel; to Tony Faust's; Specks, which was German; Mertika Jim's, dispensing superb Greek food; Schumacher's, famed for its catfish and turtle soup.

There is a wealth of worthy restaurants from which to choose for the present-day St. Louisan as well. This book presents only 21 of those—a difficult choice, indeed—but even so, as a perennial weight watcher, I knew it would be impossible to properly "research" this assignment alone (although I must say that in almost every restaurant represented, the selective dieter can be quite comfortable with his choices). Long an admirer of the *haute cuisine* of Ceci Lowenhaupt, I called upon her to co-author "Dining In St. Louis." She accepted the challenge and has been responsible for much of the work that has gone into this book . . . a restaurant guide and cookbook in one.

Visitors—drawn to St. Louis to view the spectacular Saarinen Arch . . . the renowned Missouri Botanical Gardens . . . our Zoo . . . the famed outdoor Municipal Opera—find this a warm and friendly city. That welcoming warmth is reinforced at our restaurants, from Busch's Grove to the tiniest of eateries all over town. Gourmet readers may be interested, incidentally, to know that John Volpi and Co., of our famous Italian Hill, produce some of the finest prosciutto in all the world. (Another bit of gastronomic lore: the first hot dog and the first ice cream cone were introduced at the fabled St. Louis World's Fair!)

To those of you who will prepare the recipes of "Dining In St. Louis," I wish the very best of good eating in your own homes. Just don't forget to tell your guests it all started in St. Louis. *Bon appetit!*

[signature] "Cabby"

LITTLE PLACE

Dinner For Six

Arancine al Burro

Costoletta alla Sherry

Involtini di Melenzane

Coppa Primavera

Caffè Mediterraneo

Wine:

With Arancine—Jaboulet-Vercherre Pouilly-Fuissé, '76
With Costoletta—Sassella Negre, '72

Agostino Gabriele, Owner/Chef di Cucina
Rosario Gabriele, Owner/Maître d'Hotel

"Ristorante Dei Buon Ricordo . . . La Buona Cucina Italiana": Restaurant of Good Memories . . . the Best Italian Cuisine. That's *Agostino's Little Place*, an extremely engaging oasis in a West County shopping center. The contrast between the plank decking of the exterior and the warm, paneled interior creates the wonderful ambiance of a small Italian cafe.

Small wonder. Agostino and his brother Rosario apprenticed at the finest restaurants and hotels in Italy. Rosario, in Palermo with the head of the Cascino family, was a professor at the foremost culinary school in Italy, Schuola Alberghiera, and Agostino was with the Cascino son as sous chef. The brothers then parted . . . Agostino to Dusseldorf and Milan; Rosario to Switzerland. Both were always training, always learning *la buona cucina.*

Four years ago the brothers opened their first *Little Place* with only eight tables. Serving the very best quality of food with the very special Gabriele attention to detail and preparation assured instantaneous success. As Agostino says, "One of the main and most important ingredients to preparing a good meal is the time."

Now, with double the tables and a much larger kitchen, Agostino is able to "create something special for the habitués who return again and again." A winning combination . . . Agostino and Rosario . . . who make you know you're dining at leisure among friends who care enough to please you.

202 EAST MANCHESTER ROAD

ARANCINE AL BURRO
RICE BALLS STUFFED WITH HAM AND CHEESE

½ pound Italian rice
1 bag saffron (12.5 cg)
¼ teaspoon salt
1 teaspoon butter
¼ cup grated Parmigiana
½ pound baked ham, julienned
½ pound Fontina cheese, julienned
2 cups bread crumbs
5" vegetable oil

1. Place rice, saffron, salt and butter in 2½ pints cold water.
2. Bring water to a boil, constantly stirring rice.
3. Once rice has boiled, turn heat to medium. Cook until water is absorbed, about 12 minutes.
4. Place rice on a flat cookie sheet to cool 2 hours. Sprinkle ⅙ cup Parmigiana on rice.
5. Mix ham, Fontina and remainder of Parmigiana.
6. Form rice balls by covering 1 heaping tablespoon of mixture with ¼" layer of rice.
7. Gently roll rice ball in a light covering of bread crumbs.
8. Preheat oil in deep fryer to 250°. Fry rice balls 3 minutes.

You can save oil to use in deep-frying eggplant. (We think Frimex is excellent.)

Continuously dipping hands in water while forming rice balls will prevent sticking.

COSTOLETTA ALLA SHERRY

6 1-pound veal chops, about 1½" thick
1 small yellow onion, julienned
½ stick butter
1 pound fresh mushrooms, thinly sliced
½ cup halved cherry tomatoes
Salt to taste
2 ounces dry sherry
1½ cups veal broth
Pepper to taste
Small bunch parsley

1. Brown chops in broiler at high heat.
2. Meanwhile, sauté onions in butter until translucent.
3. Add mushrooms and tomatoes.
4. Place lightly salted chops into pan; add sherry, then veal broth.
5. Sauté chops on medium heat until sauce thickens, about 5 minutes.
6. Pepper to taste.
7. Serve chops on heated platter with sauce, garnished with parsley sprigs.

INVOLTINI DI MELENZANE
ROLLED EGGPLANT

1 large eggplant—as black as possible
Salted cold water
Vegetable oil
12 slices Swiss cheese
2 cooked carrots, sliced
2 hard-cooked eggs, sliced
¼ cup grated Parmigiana
Tomato Sauce
Chopped parsley

1. Preheat oven to 300°.
2. Slice eggplant into 12 pieces, ¼" thick. Soak slices in cold, salted water 2 hours, then remove from water and dry well.
3. Preheat oil in deep fryer to 250°. Lightly brown eggplant slices on both sides—about 1 minute for each side.
4. Drain on paper towels to remove excess oil.
5. Place the following on each slice: 1 slice Swiss cheese (do not allow cheese to overlap eggplant), 2 slices carrot, 1 slice egg, a sprinkle of Parmigiana, 1 teaspoon **Tomato Sauce.**
6. Gently roll eggplant by starting on 1 side and rolling to the opposite side.
7. Cover bottom of baking dish with **Tomato Sauce.**
8. Arrange rolled eggplant in baking dish, and sprinkle with Parmigiana.
9. Bake 10 minutes. Serve on warm platter, garnished with parsley.

Tomato Sauce

1 clove garlic
¼ cup olive oil
1 No.2 can whole tomatoes
Salt and pepper to taste
5 leaves fresh basil

1. Sauté garlic in oil until translucent. Remove garlic from pan.
2. Purée tomatoes in blender until smooth.
3. Add tomatoes to pan with salt, pepper and basil.
4. Simmer 20 minutes.

COPPA PRIMAVERA

2 apples, peeled and diced
2 pears, peeled and diced
2 bananas, sliced
2 oranges, cut in half sections
3 ounces white wine
½ ounce Strega
Sugar to taste
Juice of ½ lemon
1 quart Neopolitan ice cream
1 cup whipped cream
6 tablespoons Grand Marnier

1. Thoroughly mix fruit, wine, Strega and sugar. Squeeze lemon juice on mixture.
2. Place 1 full scoop of ice cream in each dessert glass. Top with half cup fruit and 1 tablespoon whipped cream for each serving.
3. At table, flambé Grand Marnier in a tablespoon. Place spoon into fruit.

Use fresh fruit only.

CAFFE MEDITERRANEO

6 cups espresso
6 ounces Cognac
3 ounces Grand Marnier
3 ounces Kahlua
6 teaspoons Triple Sec
1½ cups whipped cream
6 maraschino cherries

1. Make 6 cups of espresso. Keep hot.
2. Flambé Cognac, Grand Marnier and Kahlua for 20 seconds.
3. Fill 6 deep cups ¾ full of espresso.
4. Add 2 ounced of flambéd liqueur to each cup, then a teaspoon of Triple Sec.
5. Top each with 2 tablespoons whipped cream and a maraschino cherry.

Al Baker

Dinner for Six

Poisson de Mer aux Champignons

Vege Salad

Fresh Lemon Sole la Soulaie

French Fried Eggplant

Chocolate Mousse

Wines:
With Champignons—Piesporter Spätlese
With Sole—Marquis de Laguiche Montrachet

Mary and Al Baker, Owners
Thomas Van Hardy, Chef

Al Baker's is truly a treat for the oenophile—with a 35,000 bottle wine cellar, surely the most complete in the St. Louis area. Not just an idle boast, this, but a carefully selected collection of marvelous vintages proudly displayed for all customers to see. As a member of the prestigious Commanderie de Bordeaux, Al closes their restaurant every July for two weeks while he and his wife Mary visit the important European vineyards to taste the excellent wines they are constantly adding to their prodigious cellar.

Holding the philosophy that "the customer must be happy, the food and service impeccable, the employees perfectly trained," the Bakers are really "married to" the restaurant. Mary joins the maitre d' at the door to greet guests, Al works back and forth between kitchen and lounge, and daughter Marcia serves as captain in the dining room. Close family surveillance and cooperation unite with thorough knowledge of meats and produce to create a distinctive gustatory experience . . . complete culinary delight!

8101 CLAYTON ROAD

POISSON DE MER AUX CHAMPIGNONS

18 large mushroom caps
1 stick butter
8 ounces frozen Alaskan crabmeat, shelled
½ medium onion, finely chopped
¼ green pepper, finely chopped
1 teaspoon lemon juice
½ cup sauterne
1 teaspoon salt
½ teaspoon pepper
½ teaspoon Louisiana Hot Sauce
½ cup seasoned bread crumbs
1 tablespoon chopped parsley
¾ cup grated Parmesan cheese
Paprika to taste

1. Preheat oven to 350°.
2. Remove stems of mushrooms. Sauté caps quickly in butter. Keep warm.
3. Melt additional butter in saucepan. Sauté crabmeat, onions and pepper, mixing well, for about 5 minutes.
4. Add lemon juice, sauterne, salt, pepper and hot sauce. Mix together and simmer 5 minutes.
5. Stir in bread crumbs, parsley and ½ cup Parmesan. Mixture should be thick.
6. Fill mushroom caps with crab mixture. Sprinkle with remaining Parmesan and paprika.
7. Bake about 10 minutes or until golden brown.

VEGE SALAD

1 head romaine, torn into bite-size pieces
1½ medium carrots, slivered
6 small radishes, slivered
1 medium Bermuda onion, chopped
1 small green pepper, chopped
3 stalks celery, chopped
1½ tomatoes, diced
1 medium cucumber, diced
1½ cups bean sprouts
½ cup raw sunflower seeds
3 tablespoons Tamari sauce
1 cup cold-pressed safflower oil
¼ cup apple vinegar
½ cup grated Parmesan cheese

1. Place first 10 ingredients in large salad bowl.
2. Add Tamari. Sprinkle with Parmesan and toss lightly.
3. Add oil and vinegar. Toss thoroughly. Serve.

This is really health food. It's been a very popular salad.

FRESH LEMON SOLE LA SOULAIE

6 10-ounce filets of sole
2 cups water
1 tablespoon lemon juice
6 tablespoons oil
Champagne Sauce
1½ cups tiny, baby shrimp

1. Preheat oven to 375°.
2. Place sole in an au gratin dish with water, lemon juice and oil.
3. Poach for about 10 minutes. Remove fish to warm platter. Discard liquid.
4. Pour **Champagne Sauce** over filets. Garnish with shrimp.

Champagne Sauce

1½ sticks butter
1 cup flour
1 teaspoon salt
1 teaspoon white pepper
1½ teaspoons Louisiana Hot Sauce
1 teaspoon lemon juice
2 cups heavy cream
1½ cups champagne
3 chicken bouillon cubes
3 beef bouillon cubes

1. Melt butter in saucepan. Stir in flour and blend well. Cook over low heat, stirring, for 5 minutes or until raw taste of flour is dispelled.
2. Add salt, pepper, hot sauce, lemon juice and cream. Mix well. Simmer about 3 minutes.
3. Slowly add champagne, mixing carefully.
4. Add bouillon cubes, stirring until a thick, creamy sauce is attained.
5. Pour over fish.

FRENCH FRIED EGGPLANT

2 medium eggplants
½ cup flour
2 eggs
1 cup milk
4 cups Italian bread crumbs (seasoned)
Vegetable oil for deep-frying

1. Peel eggplant. Cut lengthwise into ½" thick sticks.
2. Soak for 30 minutes in cold salted water.
3. Remove and dry thoroughly. Roll in flour. Dip in egg wash of slightly beaten eggs and milk. Roll in bread crumbs.
4. Deep-fry until golden brown. Serve at once.

Eggplant sticks should resemble large French fried potatoes.

CHOCOLATE MOUSSE

1 8-ounce box semi-sweet chocolate
3½ tablespoons butter
3 eggs, separated
¼ cup Kahlua
1 teaspoon instant coffee
1 teaspoon hot water
¼ cup cup sugar
2½ cups whipping cream
¼ cup raw pistachio nuts, chopped
3 tablespoons Grand Marnier

1. Melt chocolate and butter in saucepan over low heat.
2. Cool chocolate mixture. Beat in egg yolks. Add Kahlua and instant coffee, dissolved in hot water.
3. Beat egg whites until stiff, gradually adding sugar.
4. Fold beaten whites into chocolate mixture until all white specks disappear.
5. Whip cream until stiff. Fold completely into above mixture, reserving ¼ cup for garnish.
6. Chill 1 hour. Scoop into sherbet glasses. Top with remaining whipped cream and pistachio nuts. Sprinkle with Grand Marnier.

Dinner for Six

Toasted Ravioli

Al's Salad

Steak Romano

Rissoto alla Milanese

Zabaglione

Wine:
Chambertin or Volnay

Albert Barroni, Owner

Between Eads Bridge and Union Electric—the river and the railroad—isolated by a thruway, is *Al's*; an old sugar warehouse, later a saloon, to quench the thirst and warm the cockles of riverboat captains, railroad engineers, coal stokers and bridge workers.

Then came Louise and Al Barroni, straight from Milan, with workmen's lunches and family dinners, a truck driver pianist and singing guests. Louise's friends made the pasta, Al brought on the steaks and Louise cooked. The guests ate it all.

A fire next door, and the old sugar warehouse was redecorated to a more prosperous taste, with overtones of Steamboat Gothic in the intimate lounge.

Young Al has carried on the traditions, however, with an abundance of excellent food and plenty of warm hospitality, serving succulent steaks and seafood. There are no menus to confuse the customer; instead, the very best raw ingredients are presented on attractively decorated platters to titillate the taste buds and arouse the appetites of the ever-satisfied diners. All this, plus one of the best wine cellars in the city.

It all adds up to *Al's* . . . the right place on the wrong side of the tracks.

FIRST AND BIDDLE STREETS

TOASTED RAVIOLI

24 frozen, bite-size ravioli
½ cup milk
2 eggs, beaten
½ cup bread crumbs
1 pint cooking oil
½ cup grated Parmesan cheese

1. Dip ravioli in batter made of milk and eggs.
2. Dredge ravioli in bread crumbs and deep fry in 350° oil 3 to 4 minutes or until they are brown and rise to the top.
3. Remove from fryer. Sprinkle liberally with Parmesan. Serve at once.

AL'S SALAD

1 medium head romaine lettuce
1 small endive
Dressing
2 hard-cooked eggs
12 shrimp, boiled
6 anchovies
12 stuffed green olives

1. Wash lettuce and dry thoroughly.
2. Toss with **Dressing**.
3. Garnish with eggs, shrimp, anchovies and green olives.

Dressing

¾ cup corn oil
¼ cup white wine vinegar
1 clove garlic, mashed
Salt and freshly ground pepper

Combine all ingredients and blend thoroughly.

STEAK ROMANO

½ clove garlic
2 cups finely ground white bread crumbs
½ teaspoon salt
¾ teaspoon white pepper
½ teaspoon paprika
¼ cup chopped parsley
½ teaspoon basil
6 10-ounce center cut tenderloins
12 ounces low-moisture, partly skimmed Provolone cheese
18 thin slices prosciutto
8 egg yolks
½ cup olive oil
½ cup beef consommé

1. Rub garlic in a mixing bowl.
2. Add bread crumbs, salt, pepper, paprika, parsley and basil;
   blend thoroughly.
3. Partially cut the tenderloins against the grain; flatten. Place 1 ounce
   cheese on each side, 3 slices of prosciutto on 1 side only.
4. Close tenderloins. Shape and mold so that each tenderloin will be
   round and of the same thickness.
5. Dip in egg yolks for about 2 minutes. Roll in bread crumbs, thoroughly
   turning on both sides and edge. Allow egg yolk to absorb enough of
   the crumb mixture to coat thoroughly.
6. Heat olive oil in skillet. Add tenderloins, cover and cook 7 or 8 minutes.
   Turn and continue to cook until done to desired degree.
7. Pour on consommé. Serve at once.

RISSOTO ALLA MILANESE

6 cups chicken stock
1 medium onion, chopped
¼ cup butter
1 cup chopped mushrooms
1 cup rice
½ cup dry white wine
¼ teaspoon saffron
½ cup Parmesan cheese

1. Bring chicken stock to a boil.
2. Sauté onion in butter until tender.
3. Add mushrooms and cook at very low temperature, stirring frequently.
4. Stir in rice and cook, stirring, until grains glisten with butter and are somewhat opaque. Add wine, stirring until evaporated. Blend in saffron.
5. Lower heat under chicken stock to simmer. Add to rice mixture a cup at a time, stirring rice after each addition, until rice is tender and nearly all stock has been used.
6. Toss with Parmesan. Serve at once.

ZABAGLIONE

5 egg yolks plus 1 whole egg
2 tablespoons sugar
½ cup Marsala wine
6 scoops vanilla ice cream
18 fresh strawberries

1. Combine egg yolks, whole egg and sugar in top of double boiler above simmering water.
2. Beat mixture with a whisk, or rotary beater, until it is pale yellow and fluffy.
3. Gradually pour in Marsala. Continue beating until the **Zabaglione** becomes thick enough to hold its shape in a spoon—perhaps as long as 10 minutes.
4. Spoon mixture into bowls or long-stemmed glasses filled with ice cream. Top with berries. Serve while still hot.

anthony's

Dinner for Six

Moules Marinière

Ris de Veau aux Morilles

Salmon Steaks with Dill

Strawberries Romanoff

Wine:
With Moules—Macon-Villages
With Sweetbreads—Meursault
With Salmon—Macon-Villages
With Strawberries—Vintage Port

Anthony and Vincent Bommarito, Owners
Peter Feranato, Chef

Just walking into the elegant *Anthony's* makes the diner feel privileged. The restaurant, designed by Gyo Obata, St. Louis's own superstar architect, is warmly contemporary, each table illuminated with its own pool of light . . . an enchanting quiet island. This aura of privacy provides the perfect setting for an important business luncheon or for a romantic *tête à tête.*

Presiding over this relaxed ambiance is Anthony Bommarito, bon vivant and teacher of Italian cuisine, completely devoted to his philosophy: "The owner-chef relationship must be good to run a fine restaurant. It takes dedication and, above all, a certain personal touch."

Chef Peter Feranato, who spent twenty-five years at Chicago's Casino Club, creates light, contemporary food characterized by Tony as "very today French-style cooking" . . . exactly suited to *Anthony's* very today, ever-satisfied clientele . . . absolutely delicious!

10 SOUTH BROADWAY

MOULES MARINIERE

5 pounds mussels, cleaned
1 cup chopped parsley
1 cup dry white wine
1 stick unsalted butter
3 tablespoons chopped shallots
1 teaspoon salt
1 teaspoon freshly ground pepper
6 tablespoons heavy cream

1. Combine everything but cream and simmer for 5 minutes.
2. Remove mussels; add cream and reduce sauce for about 5 minutes.
3. Return mussels to pot to heat. Remove and serve at once, garnished with chopped parsley.

RIS DE VEAU AUX MORILLES

3 pair sweetbreads
½ teaspoon salt
3 or 4 white peppercorns
2 teaspoons vinegar
2 small bay leaves
1 clove
½ cup flour
3 tablespoons butter
2 teaspoons chopped shallots
1 4-ounce can morels
1 tablespoon brandy
2 tablespoons dry white wine
¾ cup heavy cream
Salt and freshly ground pepper to taste
1 teaspoon chopped parsley

1. Poach sweetbreads about 8 minutes in salted water with peppercorns, vinegar, bay leaves and clove.
2. Drain; plunge in cold water to cool. Remove tendons.
3. Cut sweetbreads into ¾" slices. Season with salt and pepper and dust with flour.
4. Heat butter. Brown sweetbreads on both sides. Add shallots and morels; cook until shallots are tender.
5. Add brandy and white wine; bring to a boil.
6. Add cream; simmer 5 minutes. Taste for seasoning.
7. Remove sweetbreads and morels to heated platter. Reduce sauce to half. Pour over sweetbreads; sprinkle with parsley and serve.

SALMON STEAK WITH DILL

2 sticks butter
1 ounce lemon juice
1 tablespoon chopped fresh dill
Salt and freshly ground pepper
6 salmon steaks
Spray fresh dill

1. Melt butter with lemon juice, dill, salt and pepper.
2. Brush both sides of salmon with butter mixture. Charcoal broil on medium heat 8 or 10 minutes.
3. Serve at once garnished with spray of fresh dill.

STRAWBERRIES ROMANOFF

3 pints strawberries, rinsed and drained
¼ cup sugar
1 ounce dark rum
1 ounce Grand Marnier
1 cup whipping cream, chilled
¼ cup yogurt
2 tablespoons sugar

1. Gently mix strawberries with sugar, rum and Grand Marnier.
2. Whip cream; combine with yogurt and 2 tablespoons sugar.
3. Fold cream mixture into strawberries. Serve in glass coupe.

Bobby's CREOLE

Dinner for Six

Shrimp Rémoulade

Crab Salad

Shrimp-Okra Gumbo

Crab and Mushroom Bobby

Bread Pudding with Brandy Sauce

Wine:
Pedrizzette Pinot Chardonnay

Barbara Walters and Robert Suberi, Proprietors

Among the more interesting proponents of regional cooking in St. Louis are Barbara Walters and Bobby Sebiri, co-proprietors of *Bobby's Creole*. Bobby, a native of Hollywood, met dyed-in-the-wool New Yorker Barbara when both were getting their Ph.D.'s at Ann Arbor—she in pharmacology, he in bio-chemistry. School palled. They decided to go to New Orleans. Once there, they became involved in the export of seafood and fish to St. Louis.

Although their combined restaurant backgrounds were negligible, their understanding of the alchemy of the kitchen was deep . . . a very important attribute for the purveyor of food to the public. Imbued with a fondness for Creole cooking, they soon moved to St. Louis.

Now, several times each week their New Orleans replacement drives in with freshly caught crab, shrimp and fish from the Gulf. These, under Barbara's guidance, are the ingredients for the delicious Creole dishes they feature. While Bobby mans the bar and greets his guests, Barbara runs the kitchen, always conscious of the cataclysm of condiments and nutrients, pots and pans.

That cognizance, combined with a very real appreciation of fine food and constant researching of new recipes, has created *Bobby's Creole* . . . a neighborhood hangout for the young and not so young. Simple, but oh so good.

6307 DELMAR BOULEVARD

SHRIMP REMOULADE

30 large shrimp, unpeeled
Shrimp and crab boil, or shrimp spices
Rémoulade Sauce
1 large head Bibb lettuce
6 lemon wedges
6 sprigs parsley

1. Put shrimp and crab boil in boiling water according to package directions. Add shrimp and boil 3 minutes. Remove shrimp immediately and chill in ice.
2. Serve with **Rémoulade Sauce**. Garnish with lettuce, lemon wedges and parsley.

Rémoulade Sauce

1 bunch scallions, chopped
1 cup diced celery
¼ cup chopped parsley
2 tablespoons creole mustard—Poupon will do
1½ tablespoons paprika
1¼ teaspoons salt
½ teaspoon black pepper
⅜ cup vinegar
1½ tablespoons lemon juice
½ teaspoon basil
¼ cup olive oil
¼ cup vegetable oil

¼ cup finely diced celery
¼ cup finely diced scallions
⅛ cup chopped parsley

1. Blend first 12 ingredients at medium speed in electric blender until puréed. Pour into stainless steel or glass bowl and add additional celery, scallions and parsley.
2. Mix well. Cover and refrigerate 1 to 2 hours.

CRAB SALAD

Marinade
1 pound lump crab meat
1 small head iceberg lettuce
Garnish of lemon wedges and parsley

Marinade

¼ cup olive oil
1½ teaspoons vinegar
1½ teaspoons sauterne
¾ teaspoon black pepper
¼ teaspoon dry mustard
⅛ teaspoon thyme
¼ teaspoon basil
1 tablespoon chopped parsley
1¼ cups minced onions
⅛ teaspoon sugar
2 tablespoons sweetened lime juice

1. In a deep stainless steel or glass bowl combine and whisk **Marinade**.
2. When **Marinade** is thoroughly mixed, add crab meat, which has been carefully picked through to remove small shells. Fold in gently.
3. Refrigerate, covered, for 6 to 12 hours.
4. Serve on lettuce leaves with lemon wedges and parsley.

*Acidic foods keep longer and fresher when stored in glass or stainless steel. Both of these cold appetizers—***Crab Salad** *and* **Shrimp Rémoulade**—*are excellent and keep well refrigerated for a few days. Take your choice.*

SHRIMP-CRAB OKRA GUMBO

½ cup vegetable oil
½ cup flour
1½ cups chopped onions
½ cup chopped green pepper
⅓ cup chopped scallions
2 cloves garlic, minced
1 cup diced tomatoes
2 pounds fresh okra, thinly sliced
1½ quarts cold water
1 tablespoon lemon juice
3 gumbo crabs, split in half
1 pound shrimp, peeled and deveined
4 whole bay leaves
1 teaspoon thyme
2 teaspoons salt
1 teaspoon black pepper
⅛ teaspoon cayenne pepper
8 whole allspice
6 whole cloves
¼ teaspoon nutmeg
2 cups boiled rice

1. Heat oil on medium heat in a heavy 4- to 6-quart pot.
2. Slowly add flour, stirring constantly.
3. Stir over low heat for 45 to 60 minutes, until a smooth, peanut butter colored roux is formed.
4. Add onion, peppers, scallions and garlic. Brown until tender, stirring often.
5. Mix in diced tomatoes and okra.
6. Add water, lemon juice, crab, half the shrimp and the seasonings.
7. Raise heat to medium and bring gumbo to low boil, stirring.
8. Lower heat. Simmer 1 to 2 hours, stirring often.
9. Add remaining shrimp 15 minutes before serving time.
10. Serve over rice in deep soup bowls.

This gumbo makes an excellent soup course as well as entrée. It will keep about five days, covered and refrigerated, in stainless steel or glass. It also freezes well.

CRAB AND MUSHROOM BOBBY

2 sticks butter
2 cups chopped scallions
¾ cup chopped fresh parsley
1 quart evaporated milk—room temperature
¾ pound Provolone cheese, grated
½ cup grated Parmesan cheese
¾ cup sherry
2 tablespoons sugar
½ teaspoon crushed red pepper
¼ teaspoon Tabasco sauce
½ teaspoon marjoram
½ teaspoon basil
½ teaspoon dry mustard
½ teaspoon ground thyme
¾ pound mushrooms, chopped
1½ pounds crab meat
¼ cup cornstarch in ½ cup cold water
12 thin slices day-old French bread
½ cup grated Swiss cheese

1. Melt butter in heavy 4-quart saucepan.
2. Add scallions and parsley, reserving 3 tablespoons. Cook until soft.
3. Slowly add milk, stirring constantly over low heat.
4. When mixture is hot, add Provolone and Parmesan. Stir until cheese is melted.
5. Stir in sherry and seasonings.
6. Add mushrooms and crab meat. Cook over low heat until mushrooms are cooked but firm.
7. Stir in cornstarch and water, cooking until mixture has thickened. Remove from heat.
8. Place 2 slices of bread in individual casserole dishes.
9. Ladle the **Crab-Mushroom Bobby** over the bread. Top with grated Swiss cheese and brown under broiler until cheese bubbles. Garnish with reserved chopped parsley. Serve at once.

We use evaporated milk because it's healthier, lighter and keeps longer in the refrigerator than cream.

BREAD PUDDING

1½ cups milk
⅓ cup raisins
Sherry
½ pound day-old French bread, broken into 1" pieces
3 cups sliced peaches, drained
3 large eggs
½ cup sugar
¼ teaspoon vanilla
½ teaspoon cinnamon
½ teaspoon nutmeg
⅛ teaspoon allspice
¼ stick margarine, melted
1 cup **Brandy Sauce**

1. Preheat oven to 350°.
2. Scald milk in heavy saucepan. Remove from heat and cool.
3. Soak raisins in enough sherry to cover for 1 hour.
4. Combine bread, peaches and raisins in large mixing bowl.
5. Meanwhile, beat eggs, sugar, vanilla, cinnamon, nutmeg and allspice until light and fluffy.
6. Add cooled milk, melted butter and egg mixture to bread and fruit. Mix thoroughly, but gently, until bread is well soaked.
7. Butter a 3-quart glass or earthenware casserole, 4" deep, and pour pudding into it.
8. Bake uncovered for 1 hour, or until a knife inserted near the edge of the casserole comes out clean. Serve warm with **Brandy Sauce**.

Brandy Sauce

3 large eggs, well beaten
¼ cup sugar
¼ teaspoon vanilla
½ stick butter, melted
¼ cup brandy
½ cup milk
⅛ teaspoon cloves

1. Combine eggs, sugar, vanilla and butter in heavy saucepan.
2. Cook over low heat, stirring constantly with a whisk, until mixture begins to thicken.
3. Remove from heat. Stir in brandy, milk and cloves.
4. Place sauce in an electric blender. Blend at high speed for 1½ minutes. Sauce should be the consistency of heavy cream.

We use margarine rather than butter in pudding, because margarine generally supplies the amount of salt needed.

Busch's Grove

Dinner for Six

Mint Juleps

Vegetable Soup

Barbecued Pork Ribs

Au Gratin Potatoes

Russ's Salad

Strawberries Grand Marnier

Marianne O'Neal and Bill Kammerer, Owners
Norman Jones, Executive Chef

Fourteen years prior to the World's Fair of 1904—when most Americans were whirling to the strains of "Meet Me in St. Louis, Louie, Meet Me at the Fair"—John Busch bought the Woodland Grove. A pleasant, 10-mile house, general store and post office since 1830 became *Busch's Grove*, featuring recipes his wife had brought over from Switzerland.

In 1908, Henry—the son of John Busch—and his friend Paul Kammerer acquired the restaurant, and thus began St. Louis's favorite gathering place. Those two gracious and genial hosts (perpetuated on a bas relief in the men's bar) dispensed good fellowship, good food and good drink to a large circle of St. Louisans, many of whom have claimed the same chairs for 35 years.

In summer, the regulars gather in "cages"—screened-in gazebos—lined up outside. Winter is the time to dine by the fireplace in the cheerful, pine-paneled great room. But whatever the weather, the welcome is always warm at the *Grove*. To countless loyal patrons, *Busch's* is *the* place!

CLAYTON AND PRICE ROADS

MINT JULEPS

This is definitely the summer specialty of the house! Recipe is for one julep; multiply by six.

2½ ounces Kentucky bourbon
½ teaspoon powdered sugar
Fresh mint
Orange slice
1 maraschino cherry
½ ounce liqueur

1. Place sugar in a 12-ounce glass. Add enough water to melt sugar.
2. Add a handful of mint leaves and crush with muddler.
3. Pack shaved ice into glass and pour in bourbon. Mix this in an up-and-down motion to thoroughly mix ingredients with ice.
4. Repack with more ice and top off with liqueur of your choice.
5. Garnish with sprig of mint, orange slice and a cherry with stem.
6. Top with a small parasol (!), if you have one.

VEGETABLE SOUP

2 quarts water
2 small cans tomato purée
1 stalk celery, cubed
3 carrots, diced
1 small onion, diced
2 pounds beef tenderloin, cubed
1 beef bone
2 bay leaves
6 pods okra
Salt and pepper to taste
Beef base
2 cups medium egg noodles
1 large can tomatoes, chopped

1. Into large stockpot put water, tomato purée, celery, carrots, onion, tenderloin, bone, bay leaves and okra.
2. Cook over moderate heat about 1 hour.
3. While mixture simmers, add salt, pepper and beef base to taste.
4. Cook noodles separately in salted water. Drain. Add noodles and tomatoes to soup. Simmer about 10 minutes. Serve.

BARBECUED RIBS

3 slabs pork ribs, not to exceed 3 pounds each
Basting Sauce
Barbecue Sauce

1. Trim excess fat and skirt off underside of ribs and peel off skin.
2. Start ribs over bed of white coals, turning constantly.
3. When ribs have been lightly browned, push coals to side of grill.
4. Close cover and allow ribs to finish cooking on opposite side of coals, approximately 1½ hours.
5. During this time, ribs must be basted with **Basting Sauce** every 15 minutes.
6. After ribs are cooked, brush with hot **Barbecue Sauce**. Heat quickly. Serve.

Basting Sauce

2 cups vinegar
1 cup vegetable oil
1 cup soy sauce

Mix ingredients.

Barbecue Sauce

1 32-ounce bottle ketchup
1 5-ounce bottle A-1 sauce
1 9-ounce jar prepared mustard

Mix ingredients.

AU GRATIN POTATOES

10 medium potatoes
¼ cup butter
4 teaspoons flour
1 cup milk, approximately
1 cup grated American cheese
¼ cup grated Parmesan cheese
Salt and pepper to taste

1. Preheat oven to 300°.
2. Peel and dice potatoes.
3. Cover with water. Bring to boil and cook until half done.
4. Drain well. Return to pot and set over low burner a few moments to "dry." Set aside.
5. Melt butter in saucepan and stir in flour. Gradually add milk to mixture to make a medium sauce—*not too thick*.
6. Place potatoes in a greased au gratin dish. Pour sauce over potatoes.
7. Add American cheese. Top with Parmesan.
8. Cook until tender and brown, about half an hour.

RUSS' SALAD

½ head romaine
½ head iceberg lettuce
Bellevue Dressing
3 ounces julienne of ham
3 ounces julienne of chicken
3 ounces julienne of American cheese
3 ounces diced, cooked shrimp

1. Wash lettuce. Break into bite-size pieces.
2. Toss with **Bellevue Dressing.**
3. Top with julienne of ham, chicken, cheese and diced shrimp.

Bellevue Dressing

3 hard-cooked eggs, finely chopped
3 cups mayonnaise
½ teaspoon garlic powder
½ cup chopped chives
½ cup milk

Mix all ingredients. Beat well.

STRAWBERRIES GRAND MARNIER

1 quart fresh strawberries
3 tablespoons brown sugar
3 ounces Grand Marnier

1. Wash and hull berries. Dry thoroughly but gently.
2. Place in sherbet glasses or bowls.
3. Sprinkle with brown sugar.
4. Pour on Grand Marnier.

Cafe
Balaban

Dinner for Six

Oysters à la Crème

Egg Salad

Sautéed Sweetbreads aux Cêpres

Honey Glazed Carrots

Balaban's Tortoni

Wine:
Côtes de Provence L'Estandon Rosé

Adelaide and Herbie Balaban, Owners/Proprietors

The very name, *Cafe Balaban*, conjures up an old Left Bank brasserie with brick and brass, smoky woods, paintings and posters and—of course—a sidewalk café. And it's all there, in midtown St. Louis, orchestrated by Herbie Balaban.

Says Adelaide, his wife: "Herbie cares about everything. He always has wanted a café. He's discerning—gives enormous attention to every detail, down to the last sprig of parsley. He has created the perfect stage setting for anyone who wants to feel rich and beautiful . . . each person who enters is magically able to be his or her perfect self."

But that's not all. Thanks to Adelaide, who again credits Herbie, their menu is short but sweet, pleasing to the palate and perfectly prepared. *Balaban's* started out seven years ago with eight bar stools and forty chairs, one waiter, one bartender and one cook. Adelaide was a social worker, practicing her culinary sorcery on the side. Eight months later she took a leave of absence from her first-chosen profession—and the social services soon lost an able motivation expert.

The *Balaban's* new sidewalk café is a glamorous addition in the French tradition: copper roof, chairs copied from the Tuileries, and a *trompe l'oeil* chef commanding the entrance. The crowds pour in and stay and stay. From breakfast croissants to midnight supper, that perfect stage is never empty.

405 NORTH EUCLID

OYSTERS A LA CREME

3 dozen fresh oysters, opened and cleaned
1 cup heavy cream, approximately
36 pats of butter, paper-thin
1 cup finely grated Parmesan cheese
1 baking sheet, covered with about ½" rock salt

1. Preheat oven to 500º.
2. Place sheet with rock salt in oven until salt is hot.
3. Put oysters in deep, rounded part of shell.
4. Cover each oyster with a pat of butter.
5. Fill shell with cream. Sprinkle liberally with Parmesan.
6. Place on salt; bake until tops are delicately brown.

EGG SALAD

6 hard-cooked eggs
6 Bibb lettuce cups
1 pound small white mushrooms
Vinaigrette
1 cup **Piquant Mayonnaise**
2 tablespoons chopped fresh parsley

1. Wipe mushrooms with a damp cloth.
2. Slice and place in shallow dish with **Vinaigrette** for several hours, turning carefully now and then.
3. When ready to serve, peel eggs. Halve horizontally. Place 2 halves cut side down on a lettuce frill. Top with **Piquant Mayonnaise.**
4. Pile equal portions of mushrooms between egg halves in center of each plate.
5. Garnish liberally with parsley.

Vinaigrette

¾ cup light olive oil
¼ cup fresh lemon juice
1 tablespoon sugar
¾ tablespoon salt
¼ teaspoon paprika
¼ teaspoon dry mustard
¼ teaspoon pepper

Combine all ingredients in glass jar and cover tightly. Shake well. Store overnight before using to marinate mushrooms.

Piquant Mayonnaise

2 egg yolks
1½ cups oil (half olive oil, half vegetable oil)
2 tablespoons Dijon mustard
½ teaspoon Tabasco sauce
½ teaspoon Worcestershire sauce
Salt, pepper and lemon juice to taste

1. Place yolks in bowl.
2. Add spices. Beat with whisk, rotary or electric beater.
3. While beating, add oil gradually.
4. Beat until thick. Adjust seasonings.

SAUTEED SWEETBREADS AUX CEPRES

3 pair medium-sized veal sweetbreads
Water to cover
1 teaspoon salt
1 tablespoon white vinegar
Bouquet garni
3 bay leaves
Flour seasoned with ½ teaspoon salt, $\frac{1}{8}$ teaspoon white pepper,
    ½ teaspoon garlic powder
1 stick salted butter
1 tablespoon lemon juice
2 ounces capers, well-drained
6 lemon wedges
Chopped parsley

1. Blanch sweetbreads in enough water to completely cover them. For each quart of water, add: 1 teaspoon salt, 1 tablespoon white vinegar, plus a bouquet garni and 3 bay leaves.
2. Bring water to boil; add sweetbreads, reduce heat and simmer 20 minutes.
3. Drain sweetbreads immediately. Plunge them into cold water.
4. With a very sharp knife remove all fat membranes and tubes.
5. Slice sweetbreads into medallions of approximately equal size.
6. Pat medallions dry. Dust lightly with seasoned flour. Melt butter and cook until browned. Add sweetbreads and lemon juice; sauté about 7 minutes.
7. Remove medallions to heated platter. Toss capers in pan juices until warm.
8. Spoon capers and butter over sweetbreads. Garnish with parsley and lemon wedges.

HONEY GLAZED CARROTS

12 medium carrots, pared and julienned into strips about ¼"x 2½"
3 tablespoons clarified butter
3 tablespoons orange juice
1½ teaspoons salt
¼ teaspoon ground ginger
¼ cup honey

1. Sauté carrots in butter about 5 minutes.
2. Combine juice, honey, salt and ginger. Pour over carrots.
3. Cook-toss over high heat until juice evaporates and carrots are glazed. Carrots should still be tender crisp. Serve.

BALABAN'S TORTONI

3 egg whites
½ cup heavy whipping cream
½ cup confectioners' sugar
1 tablespoon sherry
½ cup sliced, toasted almonds
1 pound almond macaroons, coarsely crumbled
6 maraschino cherries

1. Beat egg whites till stiff, but not dry.
2. Whip cream. When firm, fold in confectioners' sugar.
3. Combine egg whites and whipped cream.
4. Fold sherry and crumbled macaroons—reserving 6 cookies for garnish—into cream mixture.
5. Spoon into glass compote or crimped tortoni paper. Sprinkle with toasted almonds. Top with maraschino cherry.
6. Freeze only until firm, not hard.
7. Serve garnished with a macaroon.

If made ahead and hard-frozen, do not add almonds and cherry before freezing. Remove from freezer twenty minutes before serving and garnish after tortoni is slightly softened. Italian Amaretti or Amarettini are perfect macaroons for this recipe.

CATFISH & CRYSTAL

Dinner for Six

Marinated Broccoli

Scotch Broth
(Lamb with Barley)

Bermuda Salad

Baked Deep Sea Whitefish

Stuffed Pork Chops

Autumn Butternut Squash

Queen of Muffins
(Blueberry)

Autumn Glow Cake

Wine:
With Soup & Broccoli—Lorenz Riesling Reserve, '76
(Alsatian)
With Whitefish—Burgess Chardonnay Sonoma, '77
With Pork Chops—Beaune Clos du Roi, '76—
Tollot-Beaut
With Cake—Braacher Himmelreich Auslese,
'76—Kesselstatt

Stephen J. Apted, Owner

Young Florence Hulling came to St. Louis in 1928 fresh from an Illinois farm. Her most ardent ambition was to open a cafeteria—not the typical quick lunch concept, but a very personalized eating place—where the regular customers would find their regular tables to which they would return day after day. For the perfect presentation of each dish, Miss Florence and her sister spent long days and frequently long evenings developing and testing new recipes.

Today, her son Steven Apted carries on her tradition of fine food, temptingly presented, in an eclectic quartet of St. Louis restaurants—vital and viable offspring of that first cafeteria still dispensing Miss Hulling's original dishes. *Catfish and Crystal*, named for Ernest Kirschten's history of St. Louis, offers Miss Hulling's delicious, traditional menus in a handsomely appointed room with elegant millwork and sparkling appointments. That—along with the *Mexican La Sala, English Cheshire Inn* and *American Open Hearth* at the Bel Air Hilton—comprise the present Hullings-Apted galaxy.

Miss Hulling's philosophy, "I love food. I love people. I want them to enjoy putting their feet under my table," still prevails.

409 NORTH ELEVENTH STREET

MARINATED BROCCOLI

1 cup white wine vinegar
¾ cup vegetable oil
1¾ teaspoons white pepper
3 teaspoons salt
1 tablespoon monosodium glutamate
4 teaspoons dill seed
1 clove fresh garlic, pressed *or* ⅛ teaspoon garlic powder
24 broccoli spears

1. Mix vinegar, oil and seasonings.
2. Be sure broccoli is cut in finger-sized servings.
3. Add to dressing and marinate in refrigerator for 24 hours. Stir once
   or twice during this period.
4. Drain well and serve.

This marinade can be re-used two or three times.

SCOTCH BROTH
LAMB BROTH WITH BARLEY

¾ pound lamb shoulder—bone in, fat trimmed
Water to cover, about 2 quarts
⅓ cup raw barley
¼ cup chopped onion
½ cup diced carrots
¾ cup sliced celery
¾ cup canned tomatoes, crushed
¾ teaspoon salt
½ teaspoon black pepper
Chopped parsley

1. Simmer lamb, covered, in 1 piece until tender, about 1½ hours.
2. Remove meat and bone from broth to cool. Save the broth. Dice meat in ½" cubes.
3. Measure broth and water to make 2 quarts. Bring to a boil, add barley, meat and vegetables and simmer until vegetables are tender and barley is cooked. Add seasonings.
4. Garnish each serving with chopped parsley.

BERMUDA SALAD BOWL

4 cups shredded lettuce
2 cups cauliflower flowerettes, sliced thin so flower shapes show
1 medium Bermuda onion, sliced thin
6 tablespoons sliced stuffed olives
Crumbled blue cheese
French Dressing

1. Lightly toss lettuce, cauliflower and onions. Heap in salad bowl or individual serving dishes.
2. Sprinkle top with olives and crumbled blue cheese.
3. Pass the **French Dressing.**

Green onions may be used when in season. Slice them, tops and all.

French Dressing

1 egg
3 tablespoons sugar
1 tablespoon salt
$\frac{1}{8}$ teaspoon garlic powder *or* 1 clove garlic, pressed
$\frac{1}{4}$ cup chopped onion
$\frac{1}{2}$ teaspoon paprika
$1\frac{1}{2}$ teaspoons dry mustard
$\frac{1}{2}$ cup cider vinegar
Dash cayenne and white pepper
2 cups salad oil

1. Using a blender, mix all ingredients together except vinegar and oil. Add vinegar.
2. Add salad oil slowly and continue blending until well mixed.

Add ¾ tablespoon tarragon vinegar if flavor is desired. This recipe makes about three cups and may be refrigerated for future use.

BAKED DEEP SEA WHITEFISH

6 5-ounce portions whitefish
6 slices stale white bread
Melted butter

1. Preheat oven to 350°.
2. Trim crust from bread. Coarsely chop trimmed bread.
3. Dip fish in melted butter. Roll in chopped bread crumbs.
4. Place in baking pan. Sprinkle lightly with salt. Bake 20 to 25 minutes. Brown very lightly under broiler.
5. Serve with **Creole Mushroom Wine Sauce.**

Creole Mushroom Wine Sauce

½ medium onion, cubed
½ medium green pepper, cubed
1 small stalk celery, cubed
1 tablespoon salad oil
1 cup sliced fresh mushrooms
¾ cup canned tomatoes, crushed
1½ teaspoons granulated sugar
¾ teaspoon salt
⅓ teaspoon black pepper
Dash Tabasco sauce
1 teaspoon cornstarch
1 tablespoon cold water
1½ tablespoons sherry

1. Sauté onion, pepper and celery in oil until transparent. Add mushrooms and sauté 3 or 4 minutes.
2. Add tomatoes and seasonings and simmer, covered, 30 minutes.
3. Dissolve cornstarch in cold water, stir into sauce and cook until clear.
4. Add sherry after sauce is cooled.

STUFFED PORK CHOPS

6 double-thick pork chops, about 2 pounds
Celery Bread Dressing
Salt and pepper to taste

1. Preheat oven to 350°.
2. Have butcher make a pocket in each chop. Fill generously with unbaked **Celery Bread Dressing** or celery apple dressing.
3. Place on baking sheet. Season with salt and pepper. Bake 1 hour.
4. If desired, make brown gravy from drippings.

Celery Bread Dressing

½ 1-pound loaf stale white bread
¾ cup chopped onion
1¾ cups chopped celery
3 tablespoons chicken fat or butter
2 tablespoons chopped parsley
3 tablespoons chipped celery leaves
1 teaspoon salt
¼ teaspoon white pepper
⅓ cup pork or chicken stock
1 slightly beaten egg

1. Preheat oven to 350°.
2. Tear bread into ½" pieces.
3. Sauté onion and celery in fat until translucent; do not brown. Cool slightly.
4. Add to bread with remaining ingredients and mix lightly, but thoroughly.
5. Pile loosely into a buttered baking pan and bake ½ hour. Loosen with a spoon and turn dressing and continue baking 15 minutes, or until top is lightly browned.
6. Serve with pork, veal or fowl.

For celery-apple dressing, replace half of the celery with cored and chopped apples. Do not peel. Wonderful with roast pork, or to use for stuffed pork chops.

We recommend baking the dressing in a separate pan for more accurate results in roasting meat or fowl.

Any leftover baked dressing can be frozen for future use.

AUTUMN BUTTERNUT SQUASH

1 medium butternut squash—about 2 pounds
2 tablespoons butter
½ tablespoon brown sugar
⅛ teaspoon salt
Pinch white pepper
2¼ teaspoons shortening
3 cups sliced Jonathan apples, about 1 pound, unpeeled
2 tablespoons sugar
Nutty Topping

1. Preheat oven to moderate: 325° or 350°.
2. Cut squash in half lengthwise. Scrape out seeds and membrane. Steam 30 minutes, or bake upside-down on foil in moderate oven until tender.
3. Scrape out pulp and mash or beat in a mixer until smooth. Season with butter, brown sugar, salt and pepper. Set aside.
4. Heat shortening in a small skillet. Add apples; sprinkle with sugar. Cover and simmer over low heat until barely tender.
5. Spread in a 9" round or 8" square casserole. Spoon squash evenly over apples.
6. Sprinkle **Nutty Topping** over the squash.
7. Bake 12 to 15 minutes or until browned. Serve piping hot.

Nutty Topping

1½ cups cornflakes, coarsely crushed
¼ cup chopped pecans
1 tablespoon melted butter
¼ cup brown sugar

Gently mix all ingredients.

Mashed Hubbard squash or sweet potatoes can be prepared in the same manner.

QUEEN OF MUFFINS

¼ cup melted butter
⅓ cup sugar
1 egg, well beaten
1½ cups sifted all-purpose flour
2½ teaspoons baking powder
½ teaspoon salt
½ cup milk
¾ cup blueberries (drained, if canned or frozen are used)

1. Preheat oven to 400°.
2. Cream butter and sugar, add egg and blend.
3. Sift dry ingredients and add alternately with milk. Mix only to combine.
4. Fold in blueberries with last amount of flour.
5. Bake in greased muffin pans 20 minutes or until done.

   Makes 12 muffins.

For variations: replace blueberries with crushed pineapple, chopped sour red cherries, bacon bits, raisins, chopped uncooked prunes or apricots.

AUTUMN GLOW CAKE
CARROT CAKE WITH CREAM CHEESE ICING

1½ cups salad oil
5 whole eggs
1 cup sugar
2⅔ cups cake flour
2 teaspoons baking powder
2 teaspoons baking soda
½ teaspoon salt
1 pound carrots, ground in food chopper
½ cup chopped pecans

1. Preheat oven to 370°.
2. Blend oil, eggs and sugar on low speed until well mixed.
3. Sift flour with baking powder, baking soda and salt, and mix on low speed until well blended.
4. Fold carrots and pecans in by hand.
5. Spread into two 9" or three 7" greased and floured pans. Bake 35 or 40 minutes or until done. Invert on cake racks to cool.
6. When cool, split the layers and ice each piece and the top and sides with **Cream Cheese Icing.**

Cream Cheese Icing

½ pound cream cheese
¼ cup butter or margarine
1 pound sifted powdered sugar
1 teaspoon vanilla

Cream all ingredients together until smooth.

This cake is very easily mixed by hand or in a mixer. We bake our cake in one large pan.

Dominic's

Dinner for Six

Stracciatella

Spinach Salad

Filetti de Pollo alla Piemontese

Bianco Mangiare

Wine:
With Salad—Corvo Salaparuta
With Chicken—Barolo

Jackie and Dominic Galati, Owners
Josephine Ferrante, Executive Chef

With pretty Jackie to greet you and handsome Dominic to seat you, you know you're in the heart of the Hill . . . St. Louis's sequestered, traditional Italian quarter—a section of specialized markets, wonderful bakeries and excellent restaurants, with *Dominic's* topping the list.

The entire family is totally involved. Jackie's mother makes all the sauces, soups, canneloni and pasta. Dominic cuts his own prime quality meat and Jackie herself concocts the delicate desserts. They all collaborate on the recipes—some from their native Sicily—others they've created themselves.

Dominic moves from the intimate dining rooms to the kitchen, "watching every tray that comes out, making sure that everything is perfect." Jackie says, "We have a tremendous drive to succeed. We aim for the highest and best. And we have a marvelous relationship with our help, most of whom have been with us since the beginning, seven years ago."

She could add that they likewise have a marvelous relationship with their guests. The joy of dining there isn't simply confined to the superlative food. It's a very special kind of hospitality combined with wonderful atmosphere in the classically-appointed dining areas.

Dominic's many awards attest to all this, including the Holiday Magazine, Mainliner and Mobil awards. In a neighborhood of fine restaurants, *Dominic's* is outstanding.

5101 WILSON AVENUE

STRACCIATELLA
SOUP

4½ cups chicken stock
3 eggs, slightly beaten
2½ tablespoons flour
½ cup grated Swiss cheese
3 tablespoons grated Parmesan cheese
Dash nutmeg
¼ teaspoon salt
6 slices bread, toasted
Chopped parsley

1. Bring 3½ cups stock to a boil. Reduce heat and simmer.
2. Combine eggs and flour. Stir in cheeses, nutmeg and salt. Gradually stir in remaining stock.
3. Stir a small amount of hot stock into egg mixture.
4. Slowly stir egg mixture into simmering stock.
5. Continue to cook, stirring constantly, until mixture thickens, about 3 to 4 minutes.
6. Remove crust from bread. Toast, then cut into quarters. Float on soup. Garnish with chopped parsley.

SPINACH SALAD

2 or 3 cups raw spinach
3 slices bacon
1 whole avocado, sliced
12 strips pimento
Salt and pepper to taste
½ cup Italian olive oil
¼ cup vinegar
1 cup crumbled Gorgonzola cheese

1. Wash spinach well, and remove stems. Dry.
2. Fry bacon crisp and then drain. Chop or crumble into small bits.
3. Toss the spinach with remaining ingredients.

FILETTI DI POLLO ALLA PIEMONTESE
BREAST OF CHICKEN

6 chicken breasts, skinned and boned
½ cup flour
1 teaspoon salt
⅓ teaspoon black pepper
6 tablespoons butter
1 cup chicken stock
¾ cup dry white wine
½ cup grated Parmesan cheese
1½ tablespoons chopped parsley

1. Place chicken breasts between 2 sheets of waxed paper. Pound to flatten.
2. Put flour, salt and pepper in a large brown paper bag. Drop several pieces of chicken into bag and shake to coat each piece with flour.
3. Melt butter in large skillet. Brown chicken. Cook until done, about 5 to 8 minutes.
4. Remove chicken to warm platter.
5. Stir stock and wine into skillet. Blend with drippings. Cook until liquid is reduced by half.
6. Pour sauce over chicken. Sprinkle with Parmesan.
7. Heat under broiler until cheese browns, about 3 to 5 minutes. Garnish with parsley.

BIANCO MANGIARE
ITALIAN CUSTARD CAKE

1 9" **Sponge Cake**
½ cup sugar
⅓ cup cornstarch
1 quart milk
1 teaspoon vanilla extract
1 teaspoon cinnamon
1 cup chocolate sprinkles
1 cup chopped pecans
½ cup maraschino cherries, chopped
Chocolate sauce—optional

1. Cut cake into ½" slices. Place 1 layer in the bottom of a 9" cake pan.
   Set aside.
2. Combine sugar and cornstarch in a saucepan. Set over medium heat.
   Add milk gradually and cook, stirring, until mixture comes to a boil
   and thickens. Remove from heat. Stir in vanilla and cinnamon.
3. Pour half the pudding over the sliced cake. Scatter over this half the
   chocolate and half the pecans.
4. Add another layer of cake, then rest of pudding and remaining chocolate
   and pecans. Top with cherries. Refrigerate.
5. Serve cold on chilled plates with chocolate sauce, if desired.

Sponge Cake

(2 9" layers)

6 eggs, separated
½ teaspoon salt
1 cup sugar
1 tablespoon water
1 cup sifted cake flour
1½ teaspoons baking powder
1 teaspoon lemon rind

1. Preheat oven to 350°.
2. Combine egg whites and salt. Beat until they stand in soft peaks.
3. Gradually beat in ¼ cup sugar.
4. In another bowl, beat egg yolks until thick and foamy. Slowly beat in remaining sugar and water.
5. Sift together flour and baking powder. Slowly add yolk mixture. Stir in lemon rind.
6. Fold egg whites into egg yolk mixture until well blended.
7. Pour into 2 9" cake pans lined with lightly floured waxed paper.
8. Bake 25 to 30 minutes or until cake springs back when lightly touched with finger. Allow to cool. Remove from pans and peel off waxed paper.

This amount serves 10 or 12.

Duff's

Dinner for Six

Ham Croquettes with Mustard Sauce

Chilled Cucumber Soup

Salad Mimosa

Autumn Lamb Pie

Fresh Green Beans with Horseradish Sauce

Ice Cream Pie

Wine:
Simi Zinfandel, '76

Ginger Carlson Mostov, Tim Kirby and
Karen Duffy, Proprietors
Ginger Carlson Mostov, Executive Chef

Take three ambitious young people—a cateress, a housewife, a student. Mix them all together and what do you get? The ingredients for one of the liveliest and most appealing restaurants on the Euclid Avenue strip.

From its modest beginning seven and one-half years ago, *Duff's World* has taken on the character of an Irish pub with one notable difference: casual though it may appear, the food is anything but—as the following recipes will illustrate. Ginger Mostov, the cateress-turned-chef, is a perfectionist, with a carefully researched cuisine. The chef d'oeuvre changes every two months, enabling *Duff's* regulars—who are myriad—the opportunity for variety and experimentation.

Nightly entertainment, coupled with weekly poetry readings, create an atmosphere both indigenous to the young and thoroughly enjoyed by their elders. Tim, Karen and Ginger have retained the early character of the building: warm, bare brick, old natural woods, touches of stained glass. The welcome mat is always out. It's a fun place to go.

392 NORTH EUCLID

HAM CROQUETTES

3 tablespoons butter
3 tablespoons onion, finely chopped
3 tablespoons flour
¾ cup chicken broth
2 egg yolks
2 cups ground ham
3 tablespoons chopped parsley
1 tablespoon Grey Poupon Mustard
Salt and pepper to taste
Vegetable oil for deep frying
Mustard Sauce

1. *Make roux:* Melt butter. Add onion and cook slowly for 5 minutes until onions are soft. Stir in flour. Cook an additional 3 minutes.
2. Slowly add broth. Cook 2 minutes on medium heat.
3. Remove from heat. Add egg yolks, beating until smooth.
4. Stir in ham, parsley, mustard, salt and pepper. Refrigerate 2 hours.
5. Shape into croquettes. Deep fry at 350° for 5 minutes.
6. Serve with **Mustard Sauce.**

Mustard Sauce

¼ cup Grey Poupon Mustard
¼ cup brown sugar
¼ cup red wine vinegar
¼ cup water
2 teaspoons cornstarch dissolved in ⅛ cup cold water

1. Heat mustard, sugar, vinegar and water, stirring to remove all lumps.
2. Add cornstarch to mustard mixture, stirring over medium heat until slightly thickened.

CHILLED CUCUMBER SOUP

1 large onion, sliced
1 clove garlic, minced
¼ cup olive oil
4 cups peeled, sliced cucumbers
3 medium potatoes, peeled and diced
2 cups chicken broth
1 cup buttermilk
1 cup peeled, seeded and diced cucumbers
3 tablespoons diced scallions or chives
Salt and pepper to taste
2 tablespoons chopped parsley
1 tablespoon grated lemon rind

1. Sauté onion and garlic in olive oil until tender.
2. Add sliced cucumbers. Sauté an additional 5 minutes.
3. Add potatoes and chicken broth. Simmer 25 minutes.
4. Purée in blender. Then add buttermilk, diced cucumbers, scallions, salt and pepper to taste. Chill overnight.
5. Serve in chilled bowls. Garnish with lemon rind and parsley.

SALAD MIMOSA

2 or 3 small heads Bibb lettuce
2 avocados
3 hard-cooked egg yolks
Dressing

1. Arrange lettuce on individual plates.
2. Lay 3 slices of avocado across lettuce.
3. Pour on **Dressing.** Put egg yolks through sieve and sprinkle over avocado.

Dressing

½ cup olive oil
⅙ cup wine vinegar
1 tablespoon dry vermouth
¼ teaspoon dry mustard
1 slight teaspoon honey
Salt and pepper to taste

Whip all ingredients together.

AUTUMN LAMB PIE

6 noisettes of lamb
1 cup olive oil
1 tablespoon rosemary
2 tablespoons minced garlic
1 lemon, juiced (retain rind and pulp)
Salt and pepper
1 pound fresh spinach
1 pound phyllo dough
2 fresh tomatoes, sliced
1½ cups grated Kasseri cheese

1. Preheat oven to 375°.
2. Rub lamb with ¼ cup olive oil, rosemary, garlic, lemon, ½ teaspoon
   salt and pepper.
3. Brown noisettes in ¼ cup olive oil. Remove to warm platter.
4. Wash spinach. Cook until just limp. Drain well. Sprinkle with ½ teaspoon
   lemon juice, salt and pepper.
5. Take 1 sheet of phyllo and fold in half lengthwise. Brush with oil.
6. Place 1 noisette on each sheet. Pile on each: 1 tomato slice, ⅙ of spinach,
   and ¼ cup grated cheese.
7. Fold dough in a triangle (like flag). Brush top and bottom generously with
   oil and bake until crisp, about 40 minutes.

FRESH GREEN BEANS WITH HORSERADISH SAUCE

1 pound fresh green beans
2 tablespoons butter
1 teaspoon lemon juice
Salt and pepper to taste
½ cup sour cream
1 tablespoon horseradish

1. Trim and cook green beans al dente in large pot of boiling water.
2. Drain well. Toss with butter, lemon juice, salt and pepper.
3. Mix sour cream and horseradish together.
4. Arrange beans on heated platter. Pour horseradish sauce across middle.

ICE CREAM PIE

Vanilla wafers, to line 9" pie plate
1 quart vanilla ice cream, softened
Chocolate Sauce

1. Line pie plate with vanilla wafers.
2. Spoon on half of softened ice cream.
3. Spread half the chocolate sauce on top.
4. Repeat with remaining ice cream and chocolate sauce.
5. Cover with plastic wrap and freeze about 4 hours until firm. Serve.

Chocolate Sauce

1 cup evaporated milk
1 cup semi-sweet chocolate chips
1 cup mini-marshmallows

1. Place all ingredients in saucepan and stir over medium heat until marshmallows are melted and sauce thickens.
2. Cool to room temperature.

Femme Osage

Dinner for Four

Cucumber Vinaigrette

Poached Salmon with Mustard Sauce

Green Beans

Strawberries with Champagne Sauce

Pat Langenberg,
Owner and Chef

Just an hour's drive from St. Louis is Washington, Missouri—site of a panoramic view of Truman's "beautiful Missouri," home of the Missouri Meerschaum . . . and home of Pat Langenberg's *Femme Osage*. This charming country inn, occupying an authentically restored antebellum residence, began serving marvelous *prix fixe* dinners in October, 1975. Here is the very French custom of dinner as entertainment.

Owner-chef Langenberg creates and serves a four-course meal on Saturdays and Sundays, with weekly menu changes. Guests may have cocktails before dinner in the first floor lounge where embroidered linen napkins and antique furniture provide the ambiance of a private dinner party. Dinner is served on the second floor in a warmly decorated room with an iron-railed balcony overlooking the wide Missouri.

Pat has studied cooking in Paris, Versailles, St. Paul de Vence and Aix-en-Provence, where she returns semi-annually to freshen her culinary ideas. She combines her knowledge of French tradition with the use of American ingredients to serve dishes of classic elegance and delicious simplicity.

430 WEST FRONT STREET
WASHINGTON

CUCUMBER VINAIGRETTE

¼ cup Dijon mustard
2 teaspoons tarragon vinegar
¾ cup corn oil
¼ cup chopped green onions
4 cucumbers, peeled, seeded and julienned
Salt and pepper

1. Mix mustard and vinegar.
2. Whisk in oil slowly.
3. Add onions.
4. Mix sauce and cucumbers. Chill until ready to serve.
5. Before serving, salt and pepper to taste.

POACHED SALMON WITH MUSTARD SAUCE

2 tablespoons butter
8 ounces mushrooms, washed and chopped
4 salmon steaks
½ cup dry white wine
Mustard Sauce

1. Preheat oven to 350°.
2. Butter an ovenproof dish.
3. Add mushrooms to cover bottom of dish; add wine and place steaks on top of mushrooms.
4. Cover with buttered wax paper.
5. Bake 20 to 25 minutes, or until done.
6. Serve with **Mustard Sauce**.

Mustard Sauce
HOLLANDAISE PLUS WHOLE MUSTARD

5 egg yolks
1 teaspoon lemon juice
Salt and pepper to taste
2 sticks butter
2 tablespoons whole mustard (Moutarde de Meaux)

1. Place yolks in blender. Add lemon juice, salt and pepper; blend.
2. Melt butter. Add to yolk mixture slowly while blender is operating.
3. Add mustard.

Make sauce at the last minute. Never allow it to sit waiting to be served.

GREEN BEANS

1½ pounds green beans
2 tablespoons butter
Salt and pepper to taste

1. Cut ends off green beans and wash.
2. Add to 2 quarts boiling salted water.
3. Boil uncovered 2 to 3 minutes or until tender.
4. Drain at once.
5. Reheat in butter, adding salt and pepper to taste.

STRAWBERRIES WITH CHAMPAGNE SAUCE

2 egg yolks
½ cup sugar
2 teaspoons cornstarch
1 cup milk
1 teaspoon vanilla
½ cup whipping cream, stiffly beaten
¼ cup champagne
1 quart strawberries, washed and thoroughly drained

1. Combine yolks, sugar and cornstarch.
2. Add milk slowly, stirring constantly.
3. Cook over medium heat until sauce coats a wooden spoon.
4. Refrigerate until cool.
5. Add vanilla, then fold in whipping cream.
6. Gently fold in champagne, then serve over strawberries.

The Jefferson Avenue Boarding House

Dinner for Six

Cream of Tomato Soup

Tossed Salad with Red Roquefort Dressing

Smothered Breast of Chicken

Italian Hill Potatoes

Glazed Turnips

Old Fashioned Apple Compote

Wine:
Aperitif—St. Raphael on Rocks
(With Orange Twist)
With Chicken— Bell Canyon Cellars Napa Valley
Fumé Blanc, '78

Richard Perry, Owner/Chef

What's a textbook publisher doing running a boarding house? Ask Richard Perry, and he'll say, "having the time of my life!" Eight years ago this "hobby cook"—as he characterizes himself—left those weighty textbooks behind and dug deep into the wealth of the St. Louis and midwestern cookbooks he had been collecting for years. These authentic, turn-of-the-century recipes became the foundation of *The Jefferson Avenue Boarding House.* The Boarding House, which started out in one room, has now grown to two floors: Victorian barroom below, attractive dining room above. The building had been a tavern since 1897, and Perry has successfully retained that nineteenth century flavor.

"Our *esprit de corps* is exceptional," says Mr. Perry. "Everyone is very enthusiastic about what he's doing. Our staff is almost 100% new to the restaurant business, and many of them have been here five or six years. Many of them are into researching new dishes on their own." This spirit is contagious. Dinner at *The Jefferson Avenue Boarding House* is always a delicious, delightful experience.

There are no menus. Upstaging the Japanese restaurateurs, Mr. Perry presents the entrées of the evening, fully prepared, handsomely garnished. A tantalizing but mouth-watering choice, the Q.E.D. of Perry's continuing research.

3265 SOUTH JEFFERSON AVENUE

CREAM OF TOMATO SOUP

4 to 5 tomatoes, or enough to make 3 cups
½ cup chopped celery
¼ cup chopped onions
2 teaspoons basil
2 teaspoons brown sugar
Rich Cream Sauce
Salt and freshly ground pepper

1. Peel and chop tomatoes
2. Simmer tomatoes with celery, onion, basil and brown sugar until vegetables are soft.
3. Meanwhile, make **Rich Cream Sauce**.
4. Purée vegetable mixture in blender.
5. Add this mixture to the cream sauce. Season with salt and pepper. Serve hot.

Rich Cream Sauce

½ cup butter, melted
½ cup flour
4½ cups warmed milk

1. Melt butter, add flour and cook gently.
2. Add warmed milk and continue to cook, stirring. *Do not boil!*

TIP: Be sure to add tomato purée to cream sauce; otherwise, mixture will curdle.

TOSSED SALAD WITH RED ROQUEFORT DRESSING

1 head iceberg lettuce
½ head romaine lettuce
¼ head endive
Red Roquefort Dressing
Seasonal vegetables, such as tomatoes, cucumbers, radishes, etc.

1. Remove core from iceberg lettuce; hold under cold running water
   until leaves separate.
2. Wash romaine and endive.
3. Refrigerate for at least 1 hour before serving. Tear into bite-size pieces.
4. Toss with **Red Roquefort Dressing**. Garnish with seasonal vegetables
   of your choice.

Red Roquefort Dressing

¼ cup minced onion
1¼ cups mayonnaise
1¼ cups Wesson oil
5 tablespoons ketchup
2½ tablespoons sugar
2½ tablespoons red wine vinegar
½ tablespoon Dijon mustard
¾ teaspoon salt
¾ teaspoon paprika
½ teaspoon celery seed
⅛ teaspoon black pepper
⅝ cup crumbled Roquefort cheese

1. Put all ingredients except cheese in mixing bowl. Stir with paddle
   until combined.
2. Add crumbled cheese and stir lightly. Refrigerate.

This dressing will keep several weeks in the refrigerator.

SMOTHERED BREAST OF CHICKEN

3 large chicken breasts, split
Flour seasoned with salt, pepper, paprika and tarragon
6 tablespoons clarified butter or cooking oil
2 cloves garlic, crushed
3 carrots, chunked
6 ribs celery, chunked
1 large onion, chunked
2 or 3 tomatoes, chopped
1 cup rich chicken stock
1 cup still rosé wine
Salt and pepper
Chopped parsley

1. Preheat oven to 350°.
2. Dip chicken breasts in seasoned flour.
3. Brown lightly in heavy skillet in butter or oil in which garlic has been browned.
4. Place chicken breasts in a baking dish and cover with carrots, celery, onions and tomato.
5. Fill dish half-full with stock and wine.
6. Cover and braise in oven for 30 to 40 minutes until done, but not dry.
7. Remove chicken and half the vegetables and keep warm.
8. Strain remaining sauce and purée vegetables in a blender.
9. Recombine purée with sauce and simmer, adding bits of butter and seasoned flour to thicken.
10. Season sauce to taste with salt and pepper. Serve over chicken breasts on a heated platter, garnished with parsley.

Be careful not to overcook chicken!

ITALIAN HILL POTATOES

24 small new potatoes
Vegetable oil for deep frying
¼ cup chopped parsley

1. Wash potatoes thoroughly. Peel ring around each potato and place in cold water.
2. Blanch in water until nearly done; test with fork to make sure potatoes are tender. Stop cooking process by running under cold water.
3. Dry potatoes. Fry in small batches until golden brown.
4. Sprinkle with parsley. Keep warm until serving time, but do not cover completely or potatoes will get soggy.

Be sure not to overcook during blanching process.

GLAZED TURNIPS

1½ pounds turnips, diced
2 tablespoons butter
6 tablespoons dark Karo syrup
¼ cup sugar
1 teaspoon cinnamon
1 teaspoon nutmeg
1 teaspoon ground cloves
¼ cup water
⅛ cup Chablis

1. Drop turnips in boiling water to cover. Simmer until tender; drain.
2. Combine remaining ingredients in saucepan. Heat to boiling. Pour over cooked turnips. Stir and serve.

OLD FASHIONED APPLE COMPOTE

6 large baking apples—Rome Beauty, McIntosh or Greening
1 cup sugar
1 cup water
Zest of 3 lemons
Fruit liqueur—Triple Sec, framboise, Calvados or kirsch
Heavy cream

1. Peel and core apples.
2. Cut into large pieces and place in pot with sugar and water.
3. Add lemon zest. Cook until apples are soft but not mushy.
4. Remove from pan and chill in glass compote.
5. Flavor with liqueur of your choice and serve in dessert cups with heavy cream.

It's important that sauce be crystal clear and apples are firm, not mushy. This is not applesauce.

KEMOLL'S

Dinner for Four

Carciofi Fritti

Paglia e Fieno

Spiedini alla Griglia

Sesame Broccoli

Insalata Siciliana

Pignolata

Wine:
With Appetizer—Corvo white
With Spiedini—Ruffino Rosatello

Frank Cusumano, Proprietor
Dora Kemoll, Executive Chef
Douglas Cusumano, Chef

To celebrate their modest beginning over 50 years ago as a confection-ary, the Kemoll family still dip chocolates at Christmas. And, as one, they carry on the traditions and recipes of Dora Kemoll's mother, who learned cooking in her native Palermo, where her sister and husband ran a taverna.

These old recipes formed the nucleus of *Kemoll's* extensive menu. Yearly, members of the family go on gastronomic tours, garnering fresh ideas in food and wine from the premier chefs of the world. There are special trips to special countries, too, which are subsequently celebrated at *Kemoll's* very popular Gourmet Nights, held weekly throughout the year.

Recently the fourth generation took over the varied and excellent cui-sine. Douglas Cusumano is now the chef. He and four cousins are main-taining the friendly service, pleasant atmosphere and delicious foods that have made *Kemoll's* the recipient of numerous awards.

4201 NORTH GRAND

CARCIOFI FRITTI
FRIED ARTICHOKES

2 fresh artichokes
½ lemon
Batter
2 cups corn oil
Salt to taste
Accent

1. Cut 1" off top of artichoke. Remove tough outer leaves. Break off the next rows of leaves just to the tender parts—about midway toward stem.
2. Cut artichoke into quarters lengthwise. Remove choke from each quarter.
3. Rub lemon over cut edges to prevent discoloring.
4. Meanwhile, make **Batter**.
5. Slice artichokes lengthwise ⅛" thick. Preheat 1" oil in skillet. Dip artichokes in batter. Fry in hot oil about 4 to 5 minutes.
6. Drain on paper towels. Season to taste with salt and Accent. Serve at once.

Batter

2 eggs
½ cup milk
1 cup flour

Mix all ingredients. Batter should be the consistency of pancake batter.

PAGLIA E FIENO

2 ounces prosciutto, cut into strips
1 tablespoon butter
3 ounces **Yellow Fettucini**
3 ounces **Pasta Verde**
½ cup cooked peas
½ cup cream
½ cup sautéed mushrooms
½ cup grated Parmesan cheese
Freshly ground black pepper

1. Sauté prosciutto in butter. Add cooked noodles, peas, cream and mushrooms.
2. Take off heat. Add Parmesan cheese, freshly ground black pepper and serve.

Yellow Fettucine

2 eggs
1 cup flour—Semolina is best

1. Beat eggs, add flour. Mix well.
2. Knead on lightly floured board, adding more flour if dough needs to be stiffer. Let stand, covered, 1 hour.
3. Roll dough very thin. Let dry about 10 minutes.
4. Cut dough into strips. Fold each end toward center. Then double. Cut through all 4 layers into ¼" strips. Place knife blade in center and shake out strands of dough.
5. Cook in boiling salted water about 2 minutes, al dente.

Pasta Verde

11-ounce package frozen spinach
1 cup flour
2 eggs

1. Prepare spinach according to directions on package.
2. Drain well. Squeeze dry.
3. Grind 2 or 3 times, using fine blade of food chopper.
4. Mix in flour and eggs. Repeat process used for making **Yellow Fettucine.**

SPIEDINI ALLA GRIGLIA

8 2-ounce veal scallops, pounded about ⅛" thick
8 paper-thin slices prosciutto
8 slices Provolone cheese, 1"x¼"
⅓ cup olive oil
¾ cup Italian bread crumbs
2 onion slices, halved
4 bay leaves

1. Preheat oven to 350°.
2. Cover each piece of veal with prosciutto and Provolone.
3. Roll and dip in olive oil and seasoned bread crumbs.
4. Thread on 6" or 8" skewer: roll of veal, onion, bay leaf, and another roll of veal.
5. Bake covered with foil about 10 minutes.
6. Place under broiler for about 1 minute.to brown.

SESAME BROCCOLI

1 bunch broccoli
¼ cup sesame seeds
½ stick butter

1. Cook broccoli al dente in a large pot of boiling water—about 8 minutes. Drain well.
2. Toast sesame seeds in butter until lightly browned.
3. Spoon over hot broccoli. Serve.

INSALATA SICILIANA

4 tomatoes, cut into small wedges
1 red onion, cut into rings
6 anchovies, cut into pieces
¼ cup olive oil
2 teaspoons oregano
Salt and freshly ground pepper to taste
4 lettuce cups

1. Toss tomatoes, onion, anchovies, oil, oregano, salt and pepper.
2. Place in lettuce cups. Serve.

PIGNOLATA

1 egg
½ teaspoon salt
1 cup flour
2 cups vegetable oil, approximately
¼ cup plus 1 tablespoon honey
¼ cup sugar
1 tablespoon crushed stick cinnamon
¾ cup almonds, toasted and chopped
1 2-ounce chocolate bar, broken into bits

1. Combine egg and salt.
2. Add enough flour to make stiff dough.
3. Roll into pencil-thin strips. Cut into ½" pieces.
4. Preheat oil (which should be approximately 1½" deep). Fry dough until golden brown. Drain well.
5. Meanwhile, bring sugar and honey to a boil and cook 5 minutes. Remove from heat.
6. Put fried bits into bowl. Pour syrup over them and sprinkle with half of cinnamon and nuts. Stir.
7. Line platter with good-quality plastic wrap. Mound bits in the shape of a honeycomb.
8. Sprinkle with remaining cinnamon, nuts and chocolate bits.

L'auberge bretonne

Dinner for Six

Panache d'Huitres à la Riec

Crème de Melon Frappé

Medaillon de Veau Celtic
aux Trois Mousses

Salade Cornouaille

Tulipe Glacée aux Framboises

Wines:

With Oyster—White Muscadet, '78
With Veal—Châteauneuf-du-Pape
With Raspberries—Château Nairac Sauternes

Monique and Marcel Keraval, Owners
Rachel and Jean Claude Guillossou, Owners
Marcel and Jean Claude, Chefs

Far from the rocky coast of Brittany, but exuding a certain Breton flavor, is the appealing series of rooms known as *L'Auberge Bretonne*. Since its inception a scant three years ago, this inviting restaurant has doubled in size and scope, attracting an ever-widening circle of admiring diners.

The chef-owners, Marcel Keraval and Jean Claude Guillossou, both from Brittany, are married to two charming Canadian sisters. Both men possess the prestigious certificate of Professional Aptitude from the French Government. Both are proficient in the classic French, as well as regional Breton, cuisine. But it is mainly the classic which is featured at *L'Auberge Bretonne*.

Marcel trained at the culinary school in Tours; Jean Claude at the two-star Perros Guiriec in Brittany. Together they present a menu *tres formidable*. In the manner of the French host, Marcel, Jean Claude and their wives are ever present to greet their guests, suggest the specials of the day and generally maintain the friendly ambiance and exceptional food which has garnered Mainliner Awards annually.

13419 CHESTERFIELD SHOPPING PLAZA

PANACHE D'HUITRES A LA RIEC
OYSTERS FIVE WAYS

30 Bluepoint oysters
1 cup grated Parmesan cheese
1 cup white bread crumbs
6 lemon wedges
Parsley
Curry Sauce, Casino, Rockefeller, Amoricaine, Leek preparations
Roux
Lobster Sauce
Fish Velouté
Rock salt

1. Preheat oven to 450°.
2. Clean oysters. Open and separate meat from shell. Place meat in
   rounded part of shell.
3. Stuff oysters with assorted preparations: 6 with **Curry Sauce**, 6 **Casino**,
   6 **Rockefeller**, 6 **Amoricaine** and 6 **Leek**.
4. Sprinkle with Parmesan and bread crumbs. Place on bed of rock salt
   and bake for 10 or 15 minutes, or until crumbs are golden brown.
5. Serve 1 of each kind, piping hot, on individual plates, with lemon wedge
   and parsley in center.

Roux—salad oil or melted butter and flour, about the consistency of
paste, used as a thickening agent.

Curry Sauce

1 tablespoon shallots
1 tablespoon butter
1 peach, peeled and puréed
2 cups **Fish Velouté**
1 teaspoon cayenne pepper
1 tablespoon curry powder
Salt and pepper to taste
Dash Tabasco sauce

1. Sauté shallots in butter.
2. Blend in peach, **Fish Velouté** and seasonings.
3. Set aside to cool.

Casino

1 strip bacon, cooked and chopped
3 tablespoons garlic butter
3 red pimientos, chopped

Mix all ingredients.

Rockefeller

2 tablespoons shallots
2 tablespoons butter
1 box frozen chopped spinach, well drained
2 tablespoons **Fish Velouté**
1 shot Pernod

1. Sauté shallots in butter.
2. Mix thawed, dried spinach with **Fish Velouté**; add shallots.
3. Add Pernod. Set aside to cool.

Amoricaine

1 cup **Lobster Sauce**
¼ cup cooked shrimp, chopped
¼ cup heavy cream

Put all ingredients in a pot. Bring to a boil. Remove from heat and set aside to cool.

Leek

⅛ cup finely chopped leeks
2 tablespoons butter
1 ounce white wine
1 cup **Fish Velouté**
¼ cup cream
1 shot Cognac

1. Sauté leeks in butter. Add wine. Reduce for 15 minutes.
2. Mix in **Fish Velouté**, cream and Cognac. When thoroughly blended, set aside to cool.

Lobster Sauce

5 lobster shells, cracked
2 tablespoons butter
2 ounces Cognac
1 carrot, diced
1 stalk celery, diced
1 onion, diced
½ leek, diced
1 clove garlic, minced
Salt and pepper to taste
½ teaspoon cayenne pepper
1 bay leaf
Pinch thyme
½ cup white wine
1 quart water
1 beef bouillon cube
1 cup heavy cream
2 ounces **Roux**

1. Sauté lobster shells in butter. Flambé with 1 ounce Cognac.
2. Add carrots, celery, onion, leek and garlic; season with salt, black pepper, cayenne pepper, bay leaf and thyme. Add wine and simmer 15 minutes.
3. Add water and bouillon cube. Cook 1 hour.
4. Strain. Bring back to a boil. Add cream and thicken with **Roux**. Stir in Cognac. Add more salt, pepper and cayenne to taste, if needed.

Fish Velouté

Fish bones and skin
1 quart water
1 carrot, diced
1 stalk celery, diced
1 onion, diced
½ leek, diced
1 bay leaf
Pinch thyme
Pinch basil
Salt and pepper to taste
2 cups heavy cream
Roux
2 ounces white wine.

1. Bring water to a boil, add fish bones and skin, carrot, celery, onion, leek and seasonings.
2. Cook 1 hour. Strain.
3. Add cream and bring back to a boil. Thicken with **Roux**. Stir in wine.

Stuffed Apples

3 apples
Dash of white wine
2 shallots
1 clove garlic, mashed
2 tablespoons butter
Salt, pepper and cayenne to taste
8 ounces crabmeat
1 ounce Cognac
1 cup fish velouté (see **Panache d'Huitres à la Riec**)
1 tablespoon roux
Puff pastry
1 egg, beaten

1. Preheat oven to 425°.
2. Peel apples. Cut in half and scoop out insides to form a bowl. Sprinkle with white wine and bake 10 minutes. Set aside to cool.
3. Sauté shallots and garlic in butter with seasonings. Add crabmeat, Cognac and fish velouté thickened with roux (½ tablespoon butter, ½ tablespoon flour). Simmer 3 minutes. Set aside to cool.
4. When cool, place crabmeat mixture in apple halves.
5. Place each apple in the center of a 5" square of puff pastry. Cover by pulling up opposite corners of square and pinching together to seal. Brush with beaten egg.
6. When ready to serve, place in 450° oven about 10 minutes or until pastry turns golden brown.

Buy one-half pound frozen puff pastry in freezer section of supermarket.

Vegetable Mousse

6 ounces mushrooms
2 carrots
3 stalks celery
6 egg yolks
9 tablespoons heavy cream
Salt and pepper to taste

1. Preheat oven to 450°.
2. In food processor, purée each vegetable separately with 2 egg yolks, 3 tablespoons cream, salt and pepper.
3. Using small molds or custard cups placed in a pan filled with 1" warm water, layer mousse as follows: mushrooms on bottom/bake 10 minutes – carrots next/bake 10 minutes – finally celery/bake 10 minutes.
4. When ready to serve, demold.

CREME DE MELON FRAPPE
COLD MELON SOUP

3 small cantaloupes
¼ cup sour cream
Juice of 2 lemons
2 ounces port wine
½ cup milk
Salt and pepper to taste
3 egg whites

1. Cut cantaloupes in half. Discard seeds. Scoop out meat. Refrigerate shells to use as bowls.
2. Put meat in food processor with sour cream, lemon juice, wine, milk, salt and pepper. Mix well. Chill.
3. When ready to serve, whip egg whites with a pinch of salt until very stiff. Place whipped whites in a pastry bag.
4. Put soup into shells. Pipe meringue to cover soup.
5. Place under 550° broiler until browned. Serve at once.

MEDAILLON DE VEAU CELTIC AUX TROIS MOUSSES
VEAL CELTIC WITH VEGETABLE MOUSSE

18 scallops of veal, pounded thin
¼ cup flour
3 tablespoons butter
1 ounce Calvados (or applejack)
2 shallots, chopped
3 mushrooms, sliced
3 tablespoons cream
Sorrel to taste
Stuffed Apples
Vegetable Mousse

1. Dust veal with flour. Sauté scallops in butter until both sides are lightly browned.
2. Flambé with Calvados or applejack. Remove veal to warm platter.
3. To remaining juices add shallots, cream, mushrooms and sorrel. Serve as sauce over veal.
4. Garnish veal with **Stuffed Apples** and **Vegetable Mousse**.

SALADE CORNOUAILLE

¼ pound spinach
2 Belgian endive
1 leek
2 stalks celery
1 turnip
2 artichoke bottoms
2 tomatoes
6 anchovies
2 hard-cooked eggs, chopped
Sauce Vinaigrette

1. Clean, dry and crisp spinach and endive.
2. Line bottom of chilled salad bowl with spinach. Arrange leaves of endive in star shape.
3. Cut leek, celery, turnip and artichoke bottoms into julienne matchsticks. Place on top of greens.
4. Garnish with 12 tomato wedges and anchovies. Sprinkle on egg.
5. Pour on **Sauce Vinaigrette.**

Sauce Vinaigrette

⅓ cup red wine vinegar
⅔ cup olive oil
1 tablespoon Dijon mustard
Juice of ½ lemon
Salt and freshly ground pepper to taste

Mix all ingredients with wire whisk.

TULIPE GLACEE AUX FRAMBOISES
RASPBERRY TULIPS

1 cup sugar
5 ounces egg whites
½ cup all-purpose flour
2 drops vanilla extract
2 drops orange extract
6 scoops vanilla ice cream
½ pint raspberries
1 ounce Grand Marnier
6 dabs whipped cream—optional

1. Preheat oven to 425°.
2. Mix sugar, egg whites, flour, vanilla and orange extract.
3. Spread batter on buttered cookie sheet in the shape of a flower with
   4 petals (1 flower per person).
4. Bake about 5 minutes, until edges turn golden brown.
5. Remove from oven. While warm, place individual pastry petals in 5"
   diameter wine glasses to form a tulip.
6. When cold, put in 1 scoop of ice cream; top with raspberries, a few
   drops of Grand Marnier and, if desired, whipped cream.

*This entire meal was recently prepared for six food connoisseurs from
New York. They said they would return, just for this dinner!*

Le Bistro

Dinner for Six

Poulpillons Froids

Salade le Bistro

Rack of Lamb

Potato Nests with Julienne Carrots

Fraises au Grand Marnier

Wine:
With Squid—Muscadet de-Sevre-et-Maine, '76
With Lamb—Châteauneuf du Pape, '75
With Strawberries—Perrier-Jouët Champagne Extra Brut

Madame et Monsieur Gilbert Andujar et Fils,
Proprietaires

Stepping into *Le Bistro* is like a trip to Marseilles, whence came Gilbert and Simone Andujar, *proprietaires*. Here is an excellence of cuisine and service dictated by Gilbert's belief that, "the three most important attributes of a fine restaurant are: quality—everything must be fresh; consistency—each dish must always be the same; service—inconspicuous but attentive."

Gilbert, who grew up in his family's restaurant in Marseilles, trained at a succession of fine dining places and clubs when he came to America. A little over a year ago he and his wife, Simone, realized their dream: *Le Bistro* opened its doors.

Simone and Gilbert designed their warm bistro themselves: a series of intimate rooms which enhance their classic preparation of fish and seafood flown in from Boston; superb chicken, beef and veal. The traditional dishes, redolent of spices from her native Provence, are Simone's own recipes . . . carefully executed by *Le Bistro's* young chef, Thomas Shaw, who trained at the Culinary School of New York.

The menu proclaims: *"Le Bistro vous souhaite une bonne soirée et un bon appetit"*—*Le Bistro* wishes you a lovely evening and a good appetite. Their many satisfied customers can happily attest to the verity of this greeting. *Bon appetit!*

.14430 SOUTH OUTER ROAD

POULPILLONS FROIDS

The second stage of Poulpillons Froids preparation can be dealt with while the sautéed squid is cooling.

SQUID:

1½ pounds small squid
¼ cup olive oil
4 shallots, chopped
2 cloves garlic, finely chopped
3 sprigs parsley, chopped
1 bay leaf, crumbled
¼ cup dry white wine

1. Clean squid. Slice into small rings.
2. Sauté rings in frying pan with remaining ingredients.
3. Strain squid; set aside to cool.

"SALAD"

3 tablespoons salad oil
1 teaspoon vinegar
Juice of ½ lemon
1 clove garlic, finely chopped to a paste
1 small red onion, minced
2 sprigs parsley, chopped
Salt and freshly ground pepper to taste
6 lemon wedges
6 sprigs parsley

4. Combine oil, vinegar, lemon juice, garlic, onion, parsley, salt and pepper in a ceramic or glass bowl.
5. Add cooled squid; toss all ingredients. Chill for 1 hour.
6. Serve cold, garnished with lemon wedge and parsley sprig on each plate.

Simone first prepared this as an appetizer for the visit of the French Consul from Chicago. He enjoyed it so much she subsequently put it on the menu.

SALADE LE BISTRO

1 head leaf lettuce
1 head Boston lettuce
Dressing
6 large mushrooms, thinly sliced
6 slices tomato

1. Toss lettuce with **Dressing.**
2. Garnish with mushrooms and tomato slices.

Dressing

1 level teaspoon dry mustard
½ teaspoon sugar
Salt and pepper, coarsely ground, to taste
Dash of Accent
2 cloves garlic, finely chopped
1 egg
½ cup corn oil
3 tablespoons vinegar
Juice of 1 lemon
½ teaspoon Lea & Perrins sauce

1. Combine all dry ingredients and chopped garlic in blender at slow speed.
2. Add egg.
3. Add, alternately, oil, vinegar, lemon juice and Lea & Perrins sauce.

RACK OF LAMB

4 heaping tablespoons Grey Poupon Mustard
1 teaspoon rosemary
1 teaspoon thyme
1 teaspoon oregano
1 teaspoon basil
1 teaspoon marjoram
1 teaspoon crushed black pepper
2 racks of lamb: 8 chops to a rack

1. Combine mustard and spices.
2. Brush mixture on racks of lamb.
3. Wrap racks in good-quality plastic wrap and marinate 24 hours.
4. Broil at 425° about 15 minutes. Outside chops will be medium, inside medium-rare.

POTATO NESTS WITH JULIENNE OF CARROTS

6 carrots, julienned
6 Idaho potatoes, shredded
Oil for deep frying

1. Boil carrots 10 minutes. Drain and set aside, keeping warm.
2. Soak shredded potatoes 30 minutes in ice water. Drain thoroughly.
3. Preheat oil to 380°.
4. While oil heats, make crisscross layers of shredded potatoes in wire potato baskets.
5. Fry each nest about 3 minutes. After draining, return to 380° fat for approximately 1 minute, and drain again.
6. Divide carrots, which have been kept warm, into nests. Serve with **Rack of Lamb**.

FRAISES AU GRAND MARNIER

3 pints fresh strawberries
Crème Chantilly
6 tablespoons Grand Marnier

1. Place washed and well-dried strawberries and **Crème Chantilly** in glass coupe.
2. Just before serving pour on Grand Marnier.

Crème Chantilly

2 cups heavy cream
3 tablespoons powdered sugar
1 teaspoon Grand Marnier

1. Pour cream into chilled bowl and beat slowly until fairly stiff.
2. Fold in powdered sugar and Grand Marnier.

Dinner for Four

Scallops Delmonico

Fresh Spinach Salad

Vitella al Vino Bianco

Italian Fried Cauliflower

Cannoli

Coffee Cappuccino

Wine:
Soave—well chilled

Gus, Angelo and Carmen Lombardo,
Owners

High on the list of St. Louis family-owned restaurants is *Lombardo's*, owned and operated by Carmen, Angelo and Gus—all sons of the original founder. *Lombardo's* started out in 1929 as a simple fruit stand. 1934 saw the emergence of a popular neighborhood place serving spaghetti, ravioli and sandwiches. A larger kitchen was added in 1952 and finally, twelve years later, the present building was built. (Amazingly, during the entire construction of this handsome northside landmark, business was carried on as usual in what is now the parking lot, where the earlier restaurant once stood.)

The jovial hosts maintain that, "knowing most of the clientele, their likes and dislikes," makes a great restaurant. Their service is extremely personal. Many of *Lombardo's* delectable dishes are prepared at tableside. The brothers divide the responsibilities: Gus in the kitchen, overseeing orders and the preparation thereof; Carmen and Angelo out in the dining rooms "greeting and seating," giving their guests the difficult choice between the Mediterranean-style patio or the elegant terrace setting of the main room. The brothers proudly proclaim the participation of the third generation: Mike, Carmen's son, makes all their delicious ravioli.

Vive Lombardo's!

RIVERVIEW AT WEST FLORISSANT BOULEVARD

SCALLOPS DELMONICO

1 green pepper, sliced
1 onion, sliced
6 ounces ham, sliced thin
6 teaspoons butter
16 sea scallops
½ cup white wine
2 ounces pimiento, sliced
Pinch salt
White pepper to taste
1 cup **White Sauce**

1. Sauté green pepper, onion and ham in butter until tender.
2. Flour scallops lightly and sauté in butter.
3. Pour off butter and add white wine, green peppers, onion, ham, pimiento, pinch of salt and white pepper and **White Sauce**.
4. Simmer 3 minutes.

Use sea scallops. Do not overcook green pepper and onion; cook only until tender.

White Sauce

½ pound butter, melted
½ cup flour
2 cups milk
Salt and white pepper to taste

1. Add flour to melted butter, stirring until smooth. Take off heat.
2. Blend in milk, stirring until completely smooth.
3. Return to heat and cook, stirring, until thickened. Add salt and white pepper to taste.

FRESH SPINACH SALAD

3 bunches spinach, carefully washed
6 fresh mushrooms, cleaned and sliced
6 ounces blue cheese
3 fresh tomatoes, sliced
6 slices bacon, fried crisp
1 ounce wine vinegar
6 ounces olive oil
Salt and pepper
Grated Romano cheese

1. Mix spinach, mushrooms, blue cheese, tomatoes and bacon.
2. Mix vinegar, oil, salt and pepper; add to the above. Toss well.
3. Serve with topping of grated cheese.

VITELLA AL VINO BIANCO

Flour
24 ounces medallions of veal, sliced thin
2 tablespoons butter
Salt and white pepper
6 fresh mushrooms, cleaned and sliced
1 cup white wine
2 cups **White Sauce**

1. Lightly flour veal and sauté in butter.
2. Sauté mushrooms in butter.
3. Pour off butter; mix veal and mushrooms with wine and salt and pepper to taste.
4. Add **White Sauce** and simmer 5 minutes.

When adding White Sauce, do not let it get too thick. Use the same White Sauce as for Scallops Delmonico.

ITALIAN FRIED CAULIFLOWER

1 large head fresh cauliflower
2 cups Italian bread crumbs
1 clove chopped garlic
½ cup olive oil
Grated Romano cheese

1. Cut cauliflower in pieces and cook in water al dente.
2. Drain cauliflower and dip in Italian bread crumbs.
3. Sauté with chopped garlic in oil until golden brown.
4. Serve with Romano cheese grated lightly over top.

Do not let oil get too hot or it will burn bread crumbs . . . and do not overcook cauliflower when boiling.

CANNOLI
SHELLS

3 cups flour
¼ cup sugar
1 teaspoon cinnamon
¼ teaspoon salt
¼ cup shortening
2 eggs, well beaten
2 tablespoons white vinegar
2 tablespoons water—optional, as needed
Oil for deep frying

1. Sift flour, sugar, cinnamon and salt into bowl.
2. Cut in shortening until size of small peas.
3. Stir in eggs. Blend vinegar in a little at a time. If dough is too dry, add a little water as needed.
4. Knead well.
5. Place rolled dough on Cannoli forms, fry at 360° until golden brown.

Cannoli Filling

3 cups ricotta cheese
1¼ cups sugar
2 teaspoons vanilla
¼ cup chocolate chips

1. Beat ricotta, sugar and vanilla until smooth.
2. Add chocolate chips.
3. Fill shells with filling and serve.

COFFEE CAPPUCCINO

2 teaspoons cappuccino
1½ ounces Grand Marnier
4 ounces hot water
Whipped cream

1. Mix cappuccino, Grand Marnier and hot water.
2. Top with whipped cream. Serve promptly.

Spiros

Dinner for Six

Spanakopita

Avgolemono Soup

Athenia Salat

Moussaka

Baklava

(Greek Coffee)

Wine:
With Appetizer—White Demestica Achaia Claus
With Entrée—Roditi Achaia Claus

The Karagiannis Family, Owners
Tom Karagiannis, Executive Chef

SPIRO'S

Gus Karagiannis brought his wife and six children to the United States in 1956 from Ioannina in northern Greece. Today the couple—with four sons and two sons-in-law—maintain and dispense the warm Greek hospitality and delicious food which so enchant visitors to their sunny homeland. In St. Louis, a city of family-owned and operated restaurants, all three *Spiro's* are notable for a very personal kind of service.

Executive chef Tom—who, incidentally, apprenticed in Greece as a silversmith—trained under John Sekalariou, former sous chef at the renowned Tony Faust's. Today, Tom's 16-year-old son Dino is assisting his father and learning the fine points of this tasty cuisine. "From the start, all of our recipes are original," says Tom; silent testimony to the excellence thereof is *St. Louis Magazine's* Best Restaurant Award, which hangs on the wall.

Brothers Larry, Spiro and Harry Karagiannis manage the three *Spiro's*—this attractively appointed haven on Watson Road, their newest venture, is Larry's responsibility. In the interests of encouraging and maintaining the excellent standards and personal service that consistently distinguish *Spiro's*, the brothers provide five worthy young men with two-year scholarships to restaurant management school while apprenticing.

3122 WATSON ROAD

SPANAKOPITA
SPINACH PIE

2 pounds spinach
¼ pound feta cheese, grated
½ cup cottage cheese
½ cup chopped parsley
Salt and white pepper to taste
3 egg yolks, beaten
3 egg whites
½ pound phyllo (pastry sheets)
3 sticks butter, melted

1. Preheat oven to 350°.
2. Clean and chop spinach and place in large mixing bowl.
3. Add feta cheese, cottage cheese, parsley and seasoning.
4. Add beaten egg yolks and mix thoroughly.
5. Beat egg whites until stiff and carefully fold into spinach mixture.
6. Grease a 9"x13" pan and place 6 phyllo leaves, overlapping, into pan, brushing each with melted butter. Be sure surface of pan is completely covered.
7. Spread spinach mixture over phyllo evenly, then cover with 6 additional individually buttered phyllo leaves.
7. Bake approximately 1 hour or until golden brown.
8. Cut in squares; serve hot.

Phyllo is available in the frozen food section of most supermarkets.

AVGOLEMONO SOUP

1 stewing hen
6 cups chicken broth
1 cup rice
Salt and white pepper to taste
3 egg whites
3 egg yolks, beaten
Juice of 1 lemon

1. Boil stewing hen until tender. Remove from broth and cool.
2. Cook rice in broth. Add salt and pepper. Remove from heat.
3. Beat egg whites until stiff; add yolks.
4. While beating well, slowly add lemon juice.
5. Continue beating while adding warm broth and rice a little at a time until most of the broth is used.
6. Pour all back into pot, adding slivers of chicken as garnish.
7. Serve warm with wedge of lemon and freshly ground pepper.

Be sure broth is warm, not boiling, otherwise eggs will curdle. Temperature should be about 120°.

ATHENIA SALAT

1 head lettuce
2 tomatoes, quartered
1 onion, sliced
1 green pepper, chopped
1 cucumber, sliced
½ cup grated feta cheese
½ cup olive oil
¼ cup wine vinegar
Salt and freshly ground pepper
6 anchovies
12 Greek olives

1. Break up lettuce into bite-size pieces; combine with tomatoes, onions, green pepper, cucumber and feta cheese.
2. Mix oil and vinegar with salt and freshly ground pepper.
3. Pour over lettuce mixture; garnish with anchovies and olives.

MOUSSAKA

1 pound chopped lamb or beef
2 medium onions, finely chopped
½ cup olive oil
1 cup water
½ cup tomato paste
2 tablespoons minced parsley
1 stick butter
Salt and pepper to taste
2 medium eggplants
2 tablespoons flour
½ cup bread crumbs
2 eggs, well beaten
½ cup grated Kasseri cheese

1. Preheat oven to 350°.
2. Saute meat and onions in olive oil.
3. When meat is well browned, add water, tomato paste, parsley, butter, salt and pepper. Simmer on low heat 1 hour, or until thickened.
4. Meanwhile, peel and cut eggplant lengthwise in ¼" slices. Sprinkle with flour and sauté in oil until golden brown.
5. Add 2 tablespoons bread crumbs to meat mixture. Mix well.
6. Butter baking dish; sprinkle with half of remaining bread crumbs.
7. Layer eggplant and meat as follows: half eggplant, then half meat paste; then eggplant and remainder of meat.
8. Spread well-beaten eggs evenly on top. Sprinkle with grated cheese and remainder of bread crumbs. Dot with butter and bake for about 30 minutes or until golden brown.

After Moussaka is baked, cut a small wedge from corner and spoon out the excess grease.

If you can't find Kasseri cheese (try imported food shops), you may substitute a salty mozzarella.

We line the Moussaka pan with thinly sliced potatoes. It's wonderful.

BAKLAVA
PINWHEELS

Prepare Syrup recipe first and set aside to cool.

1 pound phyllo
1 pound chopped pecans (4 cups)
1 pound butter
Grated rind of 1 orange
2 teaspoons cinnamon
Syrup

1. Preheat oven to 350°.
2. Combine nuts, orange zest and cinnamon.
3. Cut phyllo leaves in half. You will then have 32 or 36 sheets. Use 8 or 9 leaves and 1 cup of nut mixture per roll.
4. To make roll: sprinkle nut mixture on first sheet; add pastry sheet and continue in this manner until 8 or 9 are used, ending with pastry sheet on top.
5. Roll tightly lengthwise and cut in 1" rolls. Arrange on cookie sheets tightly, cut side down.
6. Use remainder of phyllo and nut mixture in the same manner.
7. Melt butter and dribble evenly over rolls.
8. Bake 40 minutes in preheated oven until golden brown.
9. Pour cooled syrup over hot rolls. Allow to stand several hours; turn rolls and let stand until served. Cut across rolls to make small wheels.

Syrup

2 cups sugar
1¼ cups water
Juice of 1 medium lemon
2 tablespoons honey
1 ounce Ouzo—optional

1. Boil sugar, water and lemon juice to a thick syrup (or 225° on a candy thermometer).
2. Mix in honey and add Ouzo if desired. Set aside to cool.

Tenderloin Room

Dinner for Six

Escargots al Soave

U.S. Senate Bean Soup

Pepperloin à la Chase-Park Plaza

Hellenic Salad
with
Hellenic Dressing
(or Hack's Dressing)

Lovash
(Sesame Flat Bread)

Fresh Strawberries Dipped in Chocolate

Wine:

With Tenderloin—Bordeaux
With Strawberries—Cherry Herring

Chase-Park Plaza Hotel, Owners
Michael Villa, Executive Chef

To step into the *Tenderloin Room* is to take a step back in time into the opulent Victorian era of ornately carved mahogany, massive brass chandeliers, gilt and marble mantlepieces. This is a series of intimate, dimly-lit dining areas underscored with thick dark carpeting strewn with bright red cabbage roses.

Acquired piecemeal over many years by Chase-Park Plaza President Harold Koplar, the arches, columns, paneling, stair rails and credenzas formerly were part and parcel of several turn-of-the-century mansions in the midtown area. They do yeoman service in the *Tenderloin Room,* giving it unique distinction in the annals of specialty rooms.

In the midst of all this splendor stands the specially-built firepit with its gigantic ventilating hood. Here is the "eye" of the *Tenderloin,* where executive chef Michael Villa prepares the fabulous charcoal grillades which attract visitors from far and wide. This is leisurely dining at its finest, surrounded by the handsome appointments of long-vanished luxury. Maitre d' Hack Ulrich presides. He has greeted presidents and kings, first ladies and queens, with grace and hospitality. The same welcome awaits you.

THE CHASE-PARK PLAZA HOTEL, LINDELL AT KINGSHIGHWAY

ESCARGOTS AL SOAVE

12 tablespoons **Snail Butter**
36 shells
36 snails
6 tablespoons bread crumbs
6 tablespoons Soave white wine

1. Preheat oven to 350º.
2. Place some snail butter in each shell.
3. Put snails in shells. Fill in snail top with snail butter. Sprinkle with bread crumbs.
4. Bake in oven about 8 minutes.
5. Before serving, sprinkle snails with white wine Soave.

Snail Butter

1 pound butter
2 cloves garlic, finely mashed
1 shallot, finely chopped
1 teaspoon chopped parsley
1 teaspoon Worcestershire sauce
Juice of ½ lemon
Dash Tabasco sauce
Salt and pepper to taste

Beat up softened butter before adding other ingredients. Taste
for seasonings.

U.S. SENATE BEAN SOUP

½ pound navy beans
6 cups water
½ pound onions, diced
½ pound celery, diced
1 ounce butter
½ gallon beef stock
½ pound ham, chopped
½ pound potatoes, sliced
Salt to taste

1. Soak beans overnight in water.
2. Sauté onions and celery lightly in butter, being careful not to let them brown.
3. Add beef stock, drained navy beans (reserving 2 cups water to add later), ham and potatoes. Simmer 3 hours.
4. Add water and salt to taste. Simmer 15 minutes.

Although the recipe as given serves twelve, we suggest you make it in this quantity for best results.

PEPPERLOIN A LA CHASE-PARK PLAZA

The Marinade and Dry Spice Mixture must be prepared ahead of time.

4-pound beef tenderloin, with chain suet and membrane removed
Marinade
Dry Spice Mixture
Mustard Sauce

1. Place tenderloin in stainless steel pan or crock. Cover with **Marinade**. Refrigerate 2 to 3 days, basting occasionally.
2. Spread **Dry Spice Mixture** evenly in a flat pan.
3. Remove tenderloin from **Marinade**. Roll it—without drying—in **Dry Spice Mixture**.
4. Sear tenderloin on both sides on hot charcoal broiler; finish over slow heat, cooking about 25 minutes.
5. Serve with warm **Mustard Sauce**.

Marinade

2 onions, sliced
1 clove garlic, crushed
2 bay leaves, crushed
¾ cup olive oil

Blend all ingredients.

Dry Spice Mixture

2 handfuls fresh black pepper, crushed
1 handful rock salt
2 bay leaves, crushed
1 clove garlic, crushed

Blend all ingredients.

It is not necessary to discard olive oil marinade; it may be used over again, until it turns rancid.

Mustard Sauce

3 tablespoons chopped onions
2 shallots, chopped
½ clove garlic, crushed
2 ounces white wine
12 sprigs parsley
1 bay leaf
1 clove
1 tablespoon brown sugar
1 cup cider vinegar
3 tablespoons dry mustard
½ cup Dijon mustard
2 cups **Demi-Glace** or brown gravy
Pinch each thyme and oregano
Dash Tabasco sauce

1. Lightly sauté onions and shallots.
2. Add remaining ingredients except Tabasco sauce; simmer for
   30 minutes.
3. Strain sauce; add dash Tabasco sauce.

Demi-Glace

2 cups beef bouillon
½ cup flour
8 tablespoons butter

1. Melt butter.
2. Slowly stir in flour. Continue cooking and stirring until brown.
3. Stirring constantly to avoid lumps, pour in bouillon. Simmer about
   30 minutes, or until well blended.

HELLENIC SALAD

⅓ head iceberg lettuce
1 head Bibb lettuce
½ head romaine lettuce
2 stalks French endive
1 green pepper, cut in strips ⅓" x 1"
½ cucumber, peeled and sliced
⅓ Spanish onion, thinly sliced rings
Hellenic Dressing
1 tomato, peeled and cut in wedges
4 ounces feta cheese
12 Greek olives (black, ripe)

1. Wash and drain lettuce and vegetables.
2. Toss first 7 ingredients in large wooden bowl with **Hellenic Dressing**.
3. Top with onion rings, tomatoes, cheese, olives and freshly ground pepper.

Hellenic Dressing

1 clove garlic
8 anchovy filets
¾ teaspoon salt
5 ounces olive oil
2 ounces cider, distilled or wine vinegar
Juice of 1 lemon
4 to 6 shakes Lea & Perrins sauce
Freshly ground pepper

1. Crush garlic clove in bowl along with anchovies and salt.
2. Add remainder of ingredients and stir slowly, but thoroughly.

As an alternate dressing, here is the creation of the Tenderloin Room's popular maitre d'... Hack Ulrich:

Hack's Special Dressing

1 clove garlic, crushed
$1/8$ teaspoon paprika
1 raw egg
3 ounces olive oil
1 ounce red wine vinegar
½ teaspoon salt
4 to 6 shakes Lea & Perrins sauce

1. Crush garlic in bowl. Rub down sides of salad bowl.
2. Add paprika and egg, then whip slowly and thoroughly.
3. Add olive oil, vinegar, salt and Lea & Perrins sauce. Mix.

If used as an alternate dressing for Hellenic Salad, crumble 2 ounces of Roquefort over tossed salad and dust with freshly ground pepper.

LOVASH
SESAME FLAT BREAD

¼ cup butter or margarine—do not use oil
1 cup water
5 cups all-purpose flour
1 package active dry yeast
2¼ teaspoons salt
¾ teaspoon granulated sugar
¼ to ½ cup water, if needed
Sesame seeds—untoasted

1. Preheat oven: gas, 350°; electric, 375°.
2. Melt butter in water. Do not boil.
3. In mixing bowl, combine flour, yeast, salt and sugar. Gradually beat in water-butter mixture. If dough seems too dry, add more water, but work dough well before adding water because dough should be fairly dry, almost tough.
4. Knead with hands until dough is smooth—this takes quite a while and a lot of effort. Cover with damp hot towel and let rise in very warm place until almost doubled—about 1 to 2 hours.
5. Spread sesame seeds on board. Divide dough into pieces about the size of golf balls.
6. Roll out dough as thin as possible over the seeds, until you can almost see through the dough. Keep remaining dough covered while working with 1 piece at a time. You can also refrigerate the dough, then roll out and bake 1 at a time as needed.
7. Place oven rack in lowest position. Bake on ungreased, preheated baking sheet, 1 at a time, until golden—about 2 to 3 minutes in gas oven, or about 13 minutes in electric oven (with heating element in top).

Serve warm—or cold—with butter . . . delicious. Great with soups, fish, anything. Serve instead of rolls with dinner.

This makes about twelve balls of dough, each of which makes a plate-size piece of flat bread.

FRESH STRAWBERRIES DIPPED IN CHOCOLATE

1 quart large strawberries
1½ pounds semi-sweet chocolate

1. Wash berries, retaining green stems. Dry thoroughly in colander.
2. Melt chocolate slowly. Do not boil.
3. Holding berry by stem, immerse in melted chocolate.
4. When completely covered, lift out; place on heavy mesh screen or cake rack.
5. Continue until all berries are coated. Refrigerate immediately until chocolate hardens.

Tony's

Dinner for Four

Caponata

Cavatelli Broccoli

Veal Piemontese

Zabaglione

Wines:
With Caponata—Kir
With Cavatelli—Castel Chivro
With Veal—Brunello di Montalcino
With Zabaglione—Asti Spumante

Vincent and Anthony Bommarito, Owners
Rico Lonati, Chef

St. Louis is very fortunate indeed to have Vincent Bommarito in its midst. One of the great restaurateurs in the country, he is unquestionably Number One in St. Louis.

He and his brother Tony started their careers in a small tavern-turned-grill left as a legacy to their mother. Over the years the two Bommarito brothers transformed this tiny neighborhood bistro into a superb, nationally renowned restaurant.

The restaurant, which is located exactly where the original bar and grill began, offers impeccable service, and a classical menu presenting perfection to the fortunate diner. As Vince aptly expresses it: "You're only as good as the last thing you do." His attention to detail is legendary. He spends as much time in the kitchen tasting and conferring with head cook Rico Lonati as he does out front, warmly greeting his guests—most of whom he knows by name.

Awards are never ending: the Mobil 5-Star given to the top twelve restaurants in the country, Holiday, Ivy, National Restaurant Hall of Fame —the list goes on and on. *Tony's* is elegant. It's exciting. It's strictly special . . . a celebration all its own.

826 NORTH BROADWAY

CAPONATA

2 medium-sized eggplants
½ cup olive oil
2 onions, chopped
1 No.2 can pear tomatoes
1 cup sliced celery
2 ounces capers, washed
2 tablespoons sugar
¼ cup wine vinegar
Salt and pepper to taste

1. Wash eggplants. Peel and cut in 1" cubes. Dry well.
2. Fry in very hot oil about 10 minutes or until soft and slightly brown. Remove eggplant and put in large saucepan.
3. Brown onion in same oil, adding a bit more if necessary.
4. When onions are golden, add tomatoes and celery; simmer 15 minutes or until celery is tender. Add capers. Add this mixture to eggplant.
5. Dissolve sugar in vinegar; add salt and pepper and heat slightly. Add to eggplant, cover; simmer about 20 minutes, stirring occasionally to distribute flavor evenly.
6. Let cool. Serve as an appetizer.

CAVATELLI BROCCOLI

2 bunches fresh broccoli–flowers only
2 pounds cavatelli
1 cup fresh mushrooms
1 cup peeled, seeded and chopped fresh tomatoes
½ cup grated Parmesan cheese
2 sticks butter
Salt and pepper

1. Boil broccoli in salted water about 5 minutes. Add cavatelli; cook until al dente.
2. Drain off about ⅔ of the water. Add sliced mushrooms, tomatoes, grated Parmesan, butter, salt and pepper. Cook a couple of minutes, until blended.

Castel Chiuro, our Italian white house wine, has a crisp flavor, slight after-taste. Good with spicy seafood dishes such as shrimp marinara or seafood pasta. A Tony exclusive.

VEAL PIEMONTESE

12 2-ounce, very thin veal scallops
Flour
2 cups sliced artichoke bottoms
1 stick butter
¾ cup white wine
¾ cup veal stock–if not available, substitute beef bouillon
3 cups heavy cream
Salt and pepper to taste
Chopped parsley

1. Lightly flour scallops. Sauté veal and artichoke bottoms in butter.
2. Pour off butter. Add white wine. Quickly reduce to half.
3. Add cream, veal stock and seasonings. Remove scallops to warm platter.
4. Reduce sauce to half. Pour over scallops. Garnish with chopped parsley.

Brunello di Montalcino is the best and longest-lived red wine of Italy. It has the right to the designation Chianti, but prefers the prestige of its own name, for which it commands the highest price. Can rarely be found in export markets. Small production.

ZABAGLIONE

8 teaspoons sugar
Few drops vanilla
1 cup Marsala wine
8 egg yolks
Dash salt
24 whole fresh strawberries
Cinnamon

1. Put sugar in top of double boiler with vanilla and wine. Stir until sugar is dissolved.
2. Add egg yolks and salt. Stir with wire whip until eggs and wine become a creamy custard.
3. Meanwhile, wash and thoroughly dry strawberries. Place in tall glass.
4. Pour custard over berries. Sprinkle lightly with cinnamon. Serve with wafers if you wish.

A perfect ending would be to accompany Zabaglione with renowned Asti Spumante.

TRADER VIC'S

Dinner for Six

Hors d'oeuvres Varié

Crab Legs Marinière
Escargot Farci
Lomi Lomi
Opihis

Winter Melon Soup Supreme

Grenadins of Veal Morel

Coconut Mousse

Tahitian Coffee

Wines:

With Hors d'oeuvres—Champagne Cocktail
With Veal: Italian Rose Chianti
or
Napa Valley Burgundy

Victor Jules Bergeron, Owner
Dubois Chen, Executive Chef

Trader Vic, that magical purveyor of Polynesian and Chinese food, made the St. Louis scene in December, 1963, under the aegis of DuBois T.C. Chen, executive chef par excellence.

The "imaginative cooking," designed by Trader Vic and executed by DuBois Chen, is among the very best in the city. In 1973, Mr. Chen, a fellow of the Academy of Chefs in America, member of Les Amis d'Escoffier, and Chef de Cuisine St. Louis, became the first St. Louis Executive Chef to be certified by the American Culinary Federation.

From Shanghai, where he was born, Mr. Chen joined the French Navy as chef aboard the flagship, LaMotte Picquet. Ten years later he became the head chef at Jimmy's Kitchen in Hong Kong.

In 1962 Trader Vic persuaded Chef Chen to go to Scottsdale. The following year he moved here . . . the first and only executive chef of *Trader Vic's, St. Louis.*

"Everyone works together like a family," says Chef Chen. To that end, Mr. Chen roams from kitchen to dining rooms, making sure that the products of his kitchen are "good to look at, good to smell, good to taste; the food must be perfect." He firmly believes his duties are: "to make the customers happy, the boss happy, the employees happy." It appears he accomplishes all three.

BEL AIR HOTEL, 333 WASHINGTON AVENUE

CRAB LEGS MARINIERE

12 medium-size crab legs
1 tablespoon clarified butter
¾ teaspoon chopped shallots
Salt and pepper to taste
½ cup white wine
1 teaspoon roux
2 tablespoons **Hollandaise Sauce**
4 dashes fresh lemon juice
1 drop Tabasco sauce

1. Sauté crab legs in butter with shallots, adding salt and pepper to taste.
2. Add wine, and poach for 2 or 3 minutes until crab legs are
   thoroughly heated.
3. Drain wine from crab legs and thicken liquid slightly with roux.
4. Mix in **Hollandaise Sauce**, lemon juice and Tabasco sauce.

Hollandaise Sauce

4 egg yolks
Dash Worcestershire sauce
Dash Tabasco sauce
Juice of 1 lemon
2 sticks butter, clarified
Salt and white pepper

1. In top of double boiler, mix beaten yolks with Worcestershire, Tabasco
   and lemon juice. Continue whipping until thick and lemon-colored.
2. Slowly add clarified butter, whipping continuously. Do not let
   yolks harden.
3. Add seasoning to taste.

Keep warm no longer than five hours.

ESCARGOTS FARCIS

12 small escargots
2 teaspoons brandy
2 cloves garlic, mashed
1 teaspoon chopped parsley
1 teaspoon chopped shallots
2 tablespoons bread crumbs
1 teaspoon Worcestershire sauce
Salt and freshly ground pepper to taste
1 stick salted butter
12 large mushroom caps

1. Marinate escargots in brandy about 1 hour.
2. Preheat oven to 400°.
3. In bowl, mix garlic, parsley, shallots, bread crumbs, Worcestershire sauce, salt and pepper with butter.
4. Wash and dry mushrooms.
5. Fill each mushroom cap with escargot; top with butter mixture.
6. Bake until brown in preheated oven. Serve immediately.

LOMI LOMI

8 ounces fresh salmon, diced
Juice of 4 limes
2 tablespoons coconut milk
1½ cups chopped fresh tomatoes—about 3
2 tablespoons chopped onions
¼ teaspoon sugar
½ teaspoon salt
½ teaspoon freshly ground pepper
3 drops Tabasco sauce

1. Marinate all ingredients except tomatoes in a stainless steel or glass bowl for 2 hours in refrigerator; mix from time to time.
2. After marinating, mix in tomatoes.
3. Serve in shell on bed of crushed ice.

OPIHIS

8 ounces scallops
Juice of 4 limes
½ teaspoon salt
½ teaspoon freshly ground pepper
3 drops Tabasco sauce
1 tablespoon sour cream
1½ tablespoons coconut milk
¾ cup chopped green onion

1. In stainless steel or glass bowl, marinate scallops, lime juice, salt, pepper and Tabasco sauce. Place in refrigerator 6 hours, mixing now and then.
2. After 6 hours, add sour cream, coconut milk and green onion.
3. Serve in shell on bed of crushed ice.

WINTER MELON SOUP SUPREME

4 pieces dried Chinese black mushrooms
1 pound winter melon
3 tablespoons diced chicken
3 tablespoons diced Smithfield ham or prosciutto
2½ tablespoons diced snow peas
 4½ cups double-strength chicken stock
2 tablespoons diced bamboo shoots
Salt and pepper to taste

1. Soak mushrooms in warm water for about 30 minutes, or until soft.
2. Peel melon. Discard seeds and stringy fibers.
3. Cut melon into strips, then into 1" squares.
4. Dice chicken, ham and peapods into ½" squares and set aside.
5. Strain mushrooms. Cut away stems. Dice.
6. In soup pot, combine chicken stock, melon, mushrooms and bamboo shoots and bring to a boil. Reduce heat; simmer 15 minutes. Season to taste.
7. Ladle soup into serving bowls. Garnish with chicken, ham and peas.

If you cannot get winter melon at Oriental grocers, use zucchini, removing all seeds.

GRENADINS OF VEAL MOREL

18 scallops of veal, pounded thin
3 tablespoons flour
Salt and pepper to taste
10 tablespoons clarified butter
2 tablespoons chopped shallots
1½ cups morel mushrooms
1 cup heavy cream
3 tablespoons white sauce
Juice of 1½ lemons
Pinch cayenne pepper
Chopped parsley

1. Dust scallops with flour, salt and pepper.
2. Sauté veal quickly, a little at a time, in 6 tablespoons butter.
3. Meanwhile, in separate frying pan, add 4 tablespoons butter, shallots, morels, cream, white sauce, lemon juice, salt and cayenne. Heat slowly.
4. Pour sauce on scallops. Sprinkle with parsley. Serve at once.

COCONUT MOUSSE

1 cup plus 6 tablespoons Trader Vic's Koko Crème
1 tablespoon unflavored gelatin
Pinch salt
3 eggs, separated
1 pint half-and-half
2 teaspoons granulated sugar
¼ pound poundcake
3 tablespoons chopped pistachio nuts

1. Combine 1 cup Koko Crème, gelatin, salt and egg yolks with half-and-half. Cook *just* until ingredients are dissolved.
2. Put in bowl in bed of ice. Chill until thickened to consistency of light cream sauce.
3. Whip egg whites until stiff. Fold in sugar.
4. Fold egg whites into batter. Pour this mixture into molds (coupe, glass, etc.).
5. Cut poundcake ¼" thick into size of bottom of mold. Place poundcake on batter and chill until firm.
6. Unmold and place on serving dish. Top with 6 tablespoons whipped Koko Crème and chopped pistachio nuts.

TAHITIAN COFFEE

6 cups coffee
6 teaspoons coconut syrup
6 ounces rum
6 tablespoons whipped cream

1. Mix first 3 ingredients.
2. Top with whipped cream.

YEN CHING

Dinner for Six

Kun Pao Shrimp

Peanut Chicken

Hoo La Beef

Steamed Rice

Sautéed Snow Peas

Glacéed Sweet Potatoes

Beverages:
Green Tea
Warm Saki

John and Virginia Pei, Owners
John Pei, Executive Chef

A little over five years ago, St. Louis first experienced the gustatory delights of true Mandarin cuisine. Responsible for this pleasant phenomenon is John Pei, a native of Shantung Province in Northern China. "There is a saying in Peking," says Mr. Pie, "that if one hopes to become a good cook, he must first become a good matchmaker. The flavors of the ingredients must be married and harmonized. For centuries many of the finest chefs of the various provinces of China migrated to Peking so that a universal Mandarin cuisine was developed. Perhaps nowhere in the world are taste, texture, color and aroma more harmoniously blended to delight your palate than in the cuisine of Peking."

Thus *Yen Ching*. With an artistry evolved from experience as busboy, waiter and cook, John Pei prepares the classic Mandarin dishes as well as those of his own devising. He also shares his extensive knowledge of Peking and Szechuan cuisine at various cooking schools throughout the area.

The Peis just opened a second restaurant in Chesterfield. Marvelously decorated with Oriental artifacts and tiles the Peis have brought back from China, *Yen Ching West* is dispensing the same gracious service and delicious fare as its elder counterpart.

1012 SOUTH BRENTWOOD

The seasoning for all of our recipes should be to your own personal taste.

KUN PAO SHRIMP

12 jumbo shrimp
Batter
1 quart corn oil, approximately
6 dry red peppers
1 teaspoon finely chopped garlic
2 tablespoons chopped green onions
2 tablespoons soy sauce
1½ tablespoons vinegar
2 level tablespoons sugar
1 teaspoon sesame oil

1. Peel and devein shrimp and dry thoroughly.
2. Butterfly shrimp: split from back but do not cut through.
3. Dip shrimp in batter.
4. Deep fry shrimp in 2" of oil about 3 minutes.
5. Preheat wok or frying pan. Put in 1 tablespoon corn oil and heat.
   Add peppers, garlic, onions, soy sauce, vinegar and sugar. Stir.
6. Add fried shrimp. Baste with sauce.
7. Pour on sesame oil. Serve at once.

Always preheat wok, then add oil. This prevents additional ingredients from sticking.

Batter

1 cup flour
½ cup cornstarch
1 egg
½ teaspoon baking powder
1 tablespoon corn oil
Water

1. Mix dry ingredients.
2. Gradually add water until mixture is consistency of pancake batter.

When preparing the shrimp, use green part of onion as well as white. The green actually has more flavor.

PEANUT CHICKEN

3 boned chicken breasts
½ cup celery chunks
½ cup onion chunks
2 tablespoons soy sauce
1 egg white
2 heaping tablespoons cornstarch
½ cup chicken broth
2 cups corn oil
3 tablespoons water
2 tablespoons roasted peanuts

1. Cut chicken in ¾" chunks.
2. Mix 1 tablespoon cornstarch and egg white with chicken.
3. Preheat wok. Add oil and heat to 250°. Put in coated chicken. Stir to separate chicken chunks. Cook 3 minutes.
4. Drain chicken. Pour off oil.
5. Stir fry onions in greased wok 1 minute. Pour in soy sauce. Stir.
6. Now add celery, chicken and broth. Boil.
7. Mix remaining tablespoon of cornstarch with water. Stir into broth mixture until thickened. Add peanuts and serve at once.

HOO LA BEEF

1 pound flank steak
1 medium onion, thinly sliced
3 tablespoons soy sauce
3 tablespoons sugar
1 tablespoon sesame oil
1 level teaspoon black pepper
2 tablespoons corn oil

1. Cut flank steak against grain ⅕" thick, 2" long.
2. Mix all ingredients except corn oil. Marinate meat 1 hour to let flavor penetrate.
3. Preheat wok. Heat corn oil. Put in marinade and beef. Stir until desired doneness is achieved.

STEAMED RICE

1 cup long grain rice
Water to cover by 1½"

1. Rinse rice. Add water. Cover tightly. Cook on high flame until water
   disappears from top of rice.
2. Simmer for about 20 to 30 minutes until tender and dry.

*Rice which adheres to bottom of pan may be fried and used as
garnish for soup.*

SAUTEED SNOW PEAS

1 pound snow peas
1 tablespoon corn oil
2 green onions, split and cut in 2" strips
1 teaspoon white wine
½ cup chicken broth
1 level teaspoon salt
1 tablespoon cornstarch
3 tablespoons water
1 teaspoon sesame oil

1. String snow peas. Blanch in salted, boiling water for 20 seconds. Drain.
2. Preheat wok. Put in corn oil. Heat. Add green onions, and stir-fry.
3. Add wine, broth, snow peas and salt. Bring to boil.
4. Mix cornstarch with water. Thicken broth mixture.
5. Add sesame oil. Serve at once.

GLACEED SWEET POTATOES

2 medium sweet potatoes
1 pint corn oil
Batter *
½ cup sugar
Bowl of ice water

1. Peel potatoes. Dice in 1" squares.
2. Preheat wok. Pour in oil, reserving 2 tablespoons. Heat to 350º.
3. Dip potatoes in batter. Deep fry 3 minutes.
4. Preheat second wok or fry pan. Heat remaining 2 tablespoons oil. Stir in sugar, continuously whipping until sugar turns to light brown syrup.
5. Put fried potatoes in syrup to coat.
6. Remove coated potatoes, dip in ice water and place on hot, greased platter. Serve immediately.

*See Kun Pao Shrimp for batter recipe.

A Collection of Gourmet Recipes
From the Finest Chefs in the Country!

If you enjoyed **Dining In—St. Louis**,
additional volumes are now available for:

Please send me the quantity checked:

____ **Dining In—Chicago**

____ **Dining In—Dallas**

____ **Dining In—Houston**

____ **Dining In—Los Angeles**

____ **Dining In—Minneapolis/St. Paul**

____ **Dining In—Monterey Peninsula**

____ **Dining In—Portland**

____ **Dining In—St. Louis**

____ **Dining In—San Francisco**

____ **Dining In—Seattle**

____ **Dining In—Toronto**

TO ORDER SEND $7.95 PLUS $1.00 POSTAGE AND HANDLING FOR EACH BOOK

ORDER FORM

B I L L   T O

name _____

address _____

city _____ state_____ zip_____

PAYMENT
☐ ENCLOSED

CHARGE
☐ TO:

Visa # _____ Exp.date _____

Master Chg.# _____ Exp.date _____

Signature_____

S H I P   T O

name _____

address_____

city _____

state & zip _____ _____

name _____

address_____

city _____

state & zip _____ _____

Peanut Butter Publishing, Peanut Butter Towers
2733 - 4th Ave. So., Seattle, WA 98134